EXAMPLES & EXPLANATIONS

Legal Research in the Digital Age

EXAMPLES & EXPLANATIONS

Legal Research in the Digital Age

DeShayla M. Strachan
Mitchell Hamline School of Law

ASPEN PUBLISHING

To contact Customer Service, email customer.service@aspenpublishing.com, call 1-800-950-5259, or mail correspondence to:

Aspen Publishing
Attn: Order Department
1 Wall Street
Burlington, MA 01803

1 2 3 4 5 6 7 8 9 0

ISBN 979-8-8920-7120-8

Library of Congress Cataloging-in-Publication Data

Names: Strachan, DeShayla M. author
Title: Legal research in the digital age / DeShayla M. Strachan.
Description: Burlington, MA : Aspen Publishing, 2025. | Series: Aspen casebook series | Includes bibliographical references and index. | Summary: "The idea of researching may not be completely foreign. Before attending law school, you may have done research for other classes and thought legal research would be relatively easy. Cases would be handed to you or at least quick to find. But after spending a short time in your research class and being asked to find a specific statute, case, or reporter number, it has become clear that legal research is much more involved than people generally realize, and it has a steep learning curve"—Provided by publisher.
Identifiers: LCCN 2025040541 (print) | LCCN 2025040542 (ebook) | ISBN 9798892071208 paperback | ISBN 9798892071215 ebook
Subjects: LCSH: Legal research—United States | Legal research—United States—Data processing | Information storage and retrieval systems—Law—United States | LCGFT: Casebooks (Law)
Classification: LCC KF242.A1 S77 2025 (print) | LCC KF242.A1 (ebook) | DDC 340.072/073—dc23/eng/20250902
LC record available at https://lccn.loc.gov/2025040541
LC ebook record available at https://lccn.loc.gov/2025040542

ABOUT ASPEN PUBLISHING

Aspen Publishing is a leading provider of legal education content and digital learning solutions in the United States and globally. Our innovative products and platforms—designed based on best practices in learning science—engage students and enhance outcomes. From textbooks and audiobooks authored by renowned experts to digital platforms and products like LEAF, Connected eBooks, Connected Quizzing, PracticePerfect, and JD-Next, we empower the next generation of legal professionals with innovative, trusted, and accessible resources.

The Aspen Casebook Series, affectionately known as the "red and black" casebooks among law faculty and students, includes hundreds of highly regarded textbooks across more than 80 disciplines. These range from foundational courses like Torts and Contracts to emerging electives such as Sustainability and the Law of Policing. Our study aids, including the popular *Examples & Explanations* series, help law students master complex topics with clarity and confidence.

Aspen's expertise extends to undergraduate education with our Paralegal, Criminal Justice, and Business Law series, offering the same hallmark quality to a broader audience. JD-Next, our groundbreaking online law school prep course and admissions test, provides a realistic preview of law school, equips students with essential skills for academic success, and evaluates their readiness for legal studies.

Aspen Publishing Is Proud to Be a UWorld Company

Since 2003, UWorld has been a global leader in developing high-quality learning tools for students preparing for high-stakes exams. With a commitment to excellence, UWorld has helped millions of students in undergraduate, graduate, and professional programs in fields such as medicine, nursing, finance, and law achieve their academic and career goals.

Founded by Chandra S. Pemmasani, M.D., during his medical residency, UWorld began focusing on medical education and has since expanded into various academic fields, including law. In 2020, UWorld launched its Legal vertical, starting with its comprehensive Multistate Bar Exam (MBE®) Question Bank, followed by the acquisition of Themis Bar Review, which integrated resources to provide a complete bar exam preparation experience. In 2024, UWorld expanded its offerings by acquiring Aspen Publishing, enhancing its suite of legal education products.

Today, UWorld offers an unparalleled range of study materials that blend active learning methods with expert content, ensuring students and educators can access the most effective resources. From bar preparation to law school success, UWorld is committed to supporting the next generation of legal professionals. Learn more at uworld.com.

To my son, my mother, and first-year law students everywhere.

Summary of Contents

Contents

About the Author

DeShayla Strachan is a Visiting Professor at Mitchell Hamline School of Law where she teaches Legal Analysis, Research and Communication. She formerly taught Advanced Legal Writing as an adjunct professor at Mercer University School of Law in the Advanced Writing Certificate Program.

DeShayla worked as a journalist for ten years before entering law school. As a newspaper reporter, she worked at various community newspapers as well as a national legal news service. She is also an adjunct professor of law at Purdue Global Law School where she teaches Civil Procedure and Legal Analysis and Writing.

Preface

Navigating legal research adds to the stress and complexity of law school for first year students. Traditionally, law students took a field trip to the law library to discover how to use indexes and find legal reporters and encyclopedias. As the world has evolved, legal research has moved almost entirely online. Legal research engines such as Westlaw and Lexis dominate the market. Artificial intelligence tools such as ChatGPT and Ghostwriter Legal AI are also changing the game.

This *Examples & Explanations* study guide will aid in understanding online research and demystify the research process. In a conversational and user-friendly way, each chapter tackles topics and steps that will inevitably be discussed in a first-year research class.

Legal research classes often require students to not only learn the main research methods but also to perform research for an open memo, appellate brief, or motion pleading. This book walks students through every step of the online research process and then brings it all together with a hypothetical in Chapter 10 that determines a legal question and follows the research process to find an answer.

Giving a nod to research methods of the past, this book offers new and conventional methods to research while implementing cutting-edge technologies. In addition to demonstrating research techniques using the most common legal research engines, it also gives a glimpse into the ways in which legal research will be assessed on the NextGen Bar Exam.

DeShayla M. Strachan

August 2025

Preface

Acknowledgments

I am very grateful to Mitchell Hamline School of Law, Mercer Law School, and Purdue Global Law School for affording me the opportunity to teach Legal Research and Writing. A special thanks to my mentor and Legal Research and Writing professor, Cathren Page. I also want to thank my warriors in the W.A.R. (Writing as Resistance) writing group, who are forever encouraging and supportive of my writing endeavors. Finally, I want to thank Aspen Publishing and its staff, especially my managing editor, Elaine Page, and development editor, Troy Froebe (CEO of The Froebe Group), as well as the anonymous reviewers who offered valuable suggestions.

Legal Research in the Digital Age

CHAPTER 1

Online Legal Research and U.S. Legal Systems

INTRODUCTION

The idea of researching may not be completely foreign. Before attending law school, you may have done research for other classes and thought legal research would be relatively easy. Cases would be handed to you or at least quick to find. But after spending a short time in your research class and being asked to find a specific statute, case, or reporter number, it has become clear that legal research is much more involved than people generally realize, and it has a steep learning curve.

Such misconceptions are common. This study guide will help guide you through the various ways to research the law, with special emphasis on using online resources. It will offer simple explanations of the hypothetical questions and concepts you may come across in a first-year legal research course. It will provide examples and explanations of possible research scenarios and step-by-step walkthroughs of some of the most important online research tools. Additionally, with the implementation of the NextGen Bar Examination in many states, the study guide will prepare you for how legal research might be tested on the exam.

For centuries, research has been done to find information. Books were the primary source of any type of research until 1993 when the internet was made public. Before that, legal research was done in law libraries and any non-legal research that needed to be done happened in a nearby library branch. Growing up, I remember going through the encyclopedias I had at home or going to the local library to find what I needed for a school report. Lawyers and law students had to read through hundreds of pages of books in order to advise their clients or do assignments. But now, with multiple sources available to the public online, the research process has become much more efficient.

But what is exactly meant by legal research? It is the process used to identify and find laws. That includes court opinions, statutes, and regulations. Legal research has been defined as the finding and assembling of authorities that bear on a question of law. Lawyers and law students conduct legal research to discover the laws that apply to their particular fact patterns or case scenarios. Judges use the research compiled by attorneys in their courtroom to make decisions on pending legal matters. They may also do their own research to verify what is cited in court or documents submitted to the court. Online legal research has been beneficial in helping to get there faster. Judges now sit on the bench and can look at their computer screen to follow along with the arguments being made and verify case information. Lawyers sit in the courtroom at counsel table with their laptops or electronic tablets in hand. These devices now hold their research.

Still, navigating the many online legal research engines as a new law student can be a daunting task. As new technology, such as artificial intelligence, is introduced and increasingly used in the legal profession, it creates yet another learning curve needed to keep up with online legal research trends. But don't worry. Even with the constant evolution of modern technology, the fundamentals of legal research remain mostly the same. That is, one must first gather information, compile the applicable laws, and ensure those laws are valid. This book aims to demystify that process and illustrate the best practices.

The Evolution of Legal Research

Before the advent of the World Wide Web, walking into a library to find information was the norm. Lawyers took photos in front of rows of books to demonstrate (or give the impression of) their legal knowledge. Law firms ordered sets of books for their law offices. When presented with a set of facts, lawyers had to decide the legal question and then find the answer in a hard copy. In the law library, attorneys and law students would look for the proper reporter, which is the set of books where particular court opinions are published. They would then read the case, analyze, and take notes about their findings. They might also look through legal encyclopedias or other publications about the law in order to learn more about a topic and find cases that could be useful. They would find statutes and regulations in sets of books housed in the law library. In addition to law firms and libraries, these heavy, hardback books were also staples in courthouses. These books were the only way to find the legal precedent needed to help a client. What is legal *precedent*? It is the prior court decisions that are considered to be the authority for deciding later cases with similar legal circumstances and requirements. Finding precedent is how lawyers predict how the court may rule in a case. It may also be used to persuade a court to rule a certain way. As you can imagine, lawyers before the rise of the internet had to consult their books frequently!

With the advancement to digital research, the process looks different but is largely the same. It just takes much less time. Attorneys and law students must still define the legal question, consider reviewing legal commentary about the issue, find cases, and analyze those cases. Now, they can do all this with only access to a computer, an internet signal, and legal research software. However, the choices of how exactly to conduct that research are different now. Instead of deciding which set of reporters and encyclopedias to purchase, one must decide on a research platform. Will a fee-based legal research database be needed? Will free resources be enough? Whatever the choice, lawyers and paralegals can now quickly find the necessary legal materials.

Just when it seemed that digital research had advanced as far as it could, enter artificial intelligence. There is now AI-enhanced legal research that is meant to advance research even more with its predictive analysis, case summaries, and customized insights. All of these options will be covered in the following chapters, but any student with a long legal career ahead should realize from this recent change that it will always be important to stay up-to-date in current methods of legal research.

THE LAY OF THE LAND—U.S. LEGAL SYSTEMS

One of the first things to consider when beginning research is jurisdiction. Legal research is done at the state level and the federal level. Each state has its own statutes and legal opinions. As such, there are many volumes of state legal materials that may be similar to federal laws but only apply to that particular state. So, determining whether your legal question is a state issue or federal issue is the first priority. One must also understand the U.S. legal system and the hierarchy of courts to properly conduct legal research on either level.

The legal system in the United States consists of two parallel structures: the state system and the federal system (see Figure 1.1). Both start with trial courts at the lowest level and end with the court of last resort at the highest level. Both systems also have an intermediate court or courts in between called appellate courts.

In the federal system, the lowest courts are called U.S. District Courts. There is at least one U.S. District Court in each state. The next level of courts is called the U.S. Courts of Appeal. There are 12 numbered federal appeals circuits, not including the District of Columbia (see Figure 1.2). The highest court in the federal system is the U.S. Supreme Court.

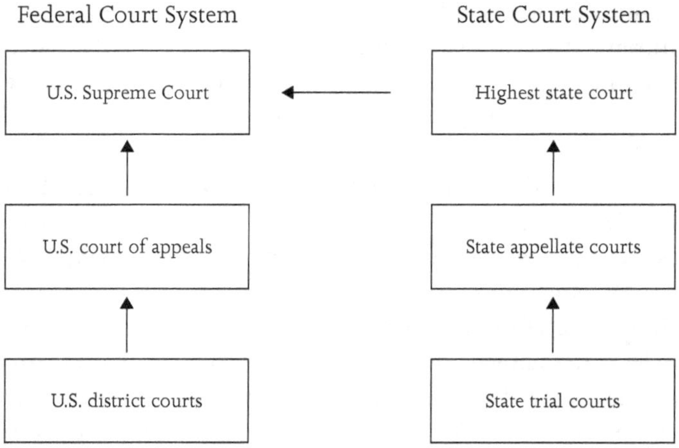

Figure 1.1 Court Systems

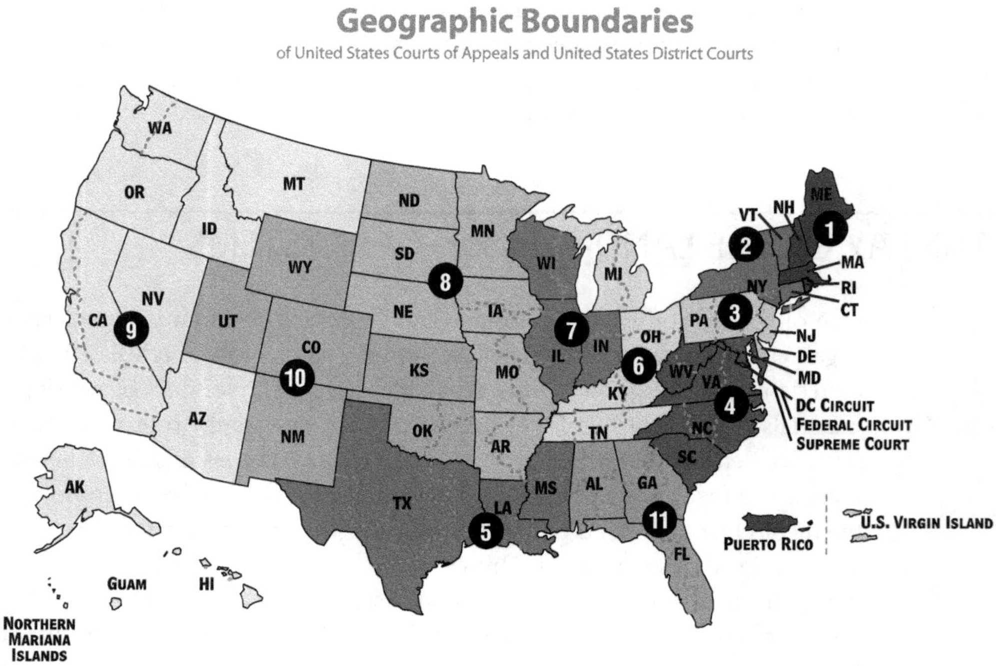

Figure 1.2 Federal Court Circuits

Source: https://www.uscourts.gov/sites/default/files/u.s._federal_courts_circuit_map_1.pdf

The state system is similar. It starts with trial courts. Most states also have intermediate courts called appellate courts. Then there is the highest court in the state, which is often called the supreme court of that state. Understanding which system you are in is key to conducting successful research. A state court decision does not have much influence over a federal court, for example, and cannot control a federal court's decision. It is critical to know where your case fits into the larger legal system of the United States to research and find appropriate legal precedent.

Stare Decisis

We talked above about how prior court decisions are considered to be an authority, which means that lower courts must follow legal precedent determined in higher courts. The legal doctrine that obligates courts to follow prior cases when making a ruling on a similar case is known as *stare decisis*, which is a Latin term meaning "to stand by things decided." The most obvious example of stare decisis is that the U.S. Supreme Court rulings govern all later rulings by lower courts in the United States. But other levels of the legal system also stand by this rule. State supreme court rulings, for example, are legal precedent for lower courts within that state but not outside the state or in federal court. There is a limited horizontal component of stare decisis that means a court will follow its own previous decisions. However, the U.S. Supreme Court has overturned its own precedent by finding that its previous ruling was made in error, so the horizontal component of stare decisis does not always work in the same way, as we will discuss below. The vertical imposition of precedent from a higher court to a lower one is more straightforward.

The purpose of stare decisis is to ensure that there is uniformity and efficiency in the justice system. The rationale here is that judges and attorneys must be able to apply the law consistently. It is also a form of judicial restraint. It prevents a judge from issuing a decision that is not aligned with previous decisions made in similar circumstances. It also ensures that all individuals are treated alike and not subject to a particular judge's personal views. Judicial precedents should govern both the same court that established the decision (horizontal component) and the courts below (vertical component).

Recent U.S. Supreme Court decisions have seemed to muddy the principles of stare decisis. There was the common assumption that a court would not go against its own prior decisions. But with the overturning of major precedent such as *Roe v. Wade* (1973) and *Planned Parenthood v. Casey* (1992) in the *Dobbs v. Jackson Women's Health* (2022) decision, law students and lawyers alike were left wondering if the role of stare decisis had been weakened.

Do not be dismayed. Precedent is still a very important part of legal research. While it will usually be helpful to predict or persuade, it must be understood that it is not always absolute. With the change in supreme court justices, in recent decisions, justices have explained that if a prior court had "poor reasoning" or was "grievously or egregiously" wrong, that may warrant the overturning of a previous decision. One justice wrote that the public must not be stuck with a bad decision due to errors in reasoning.

In *Dobbs*, Justice Samuel Alito wrote that when it comes to interpreting the Constitution, the court places high value in having matters "settled right." So, precedent is still well respected but also has a possibility of being overturned if a court deems a previous decision was improperly decided. When a case is overruled on an issue, it is no longer considered "good law." That means, it cannot be cited as controlling authority on the issue that was overturned. When reviewing cases in the research process, one of the first things to check is whether the case is still good law before relying on it in your case.

We will return to all of the above issues in the following chapters as we learn the ins and outs of legal research. Keep an eye out for the concepts we've just discussed, such as precedent and stare decisis, and before long these elements of legal research will be second nature to you.

Examples

EXAMPLES

1. While volunteering in the legal department for a local nonprofit organization, you are asked to find helpful cases for an upcoming child welfare case where a mother abandoned her child. The mother and child are located in Tennessee, and the case will be heard in state court there. Which case would be most helpful and follow stare decisis?
   a. Georgia Supreme Court cases that find a child dependent on the state for abandonment
   b. A case from an Arizona appeals court where the court found no abandonment
   c. A Tennessee appeals court case that defines abandonment in certain situations
   d. Any case with the exact same set of facts will do

2. In a case involving a criminal Illinois state issue decided in an Illinois state court, which court would be the correct place to appeal?
   a. The U.S. Supreme Court
   b. The Illinois state court of appeals in that district
   c. The Illinois State Supreme Court
   d. The U.S. District Court in Illinois

Explanations

1. (a.) Incorrect. The Georgia case may be persuasive to the Tennessee court hearing the case but according to stare decisis, the court will not have to follow it. (b.) Incorrect. This answer is incorrect for the same reason. **(c.) Correct.** This is the best answer. Because the case involves a mother and child living in Tennessee at the time of the alleged abandonment, the jurisdiction is Tennessee. Therefore, a high court in that state would be binding on lower courts in the same state. (d.) Incorrect. Cases with the same set of facts will definitely be persuasive. But unless they are from a higher court in the same state, they are not binding and do not demonstrate stare decisis.

2. (a.) Incorrect. The U.S. Supreme Court primarily hears cases involving federal issues. There is only a state issue here. **(b.) Correct.** This is the best and only correct answer. State law issues decided in state courts are appealed to the appropriate state court of appeals. Here, because there is a state issue in a state court, the proper place to appeal would be the state court of appeals. (c.) Incorrect. The state supreme court is the court of last resort. A case would not be appealed from the state court directly to the supreme court. It would be heard in an intermediate court first. (d.) Incorrect. The U.S. District Court is a federal trial court. State court decisions involving state issues are not appealed in any federal court.

CHAPTER 2

Law Gathering: Primary Sources

PRIMARY SOURCES AND WEIGHT OF AUTHORITY

Primary sources are what you think of when you think about the law. They are actual laws created by courts or legislative bodies. Case law, statutes, court rules, and other rules and regulations are primary sources. These sources are the main object of legal analysis. Primary sources are law and should be cited first, above other sources that discuss the law but are not the law. Primary sources are used in legal memos, appellate briefs, client communications, and oral arguments. Anything relating to the law other than primary sources is known as a secondary source. Secondary sources explain or comment on the law. More on those sources in the next chapter.

WHAT'S YOUR AUTHORITY?

Authority is a term often used by courts and practitioners to describe legal rules or information. When a judge or attorney asks, "What's your authority?" they are asking what source you are relying on to get to your statement of law. Is it a court case, statute, ordinance, or some other publication about the law? Primary authority refers to a source that is the rule of law, which could be binding on a court due to stare decisis. As we discussed in Chapter 1, this is the concept that when a court has already decided an issue, lower courts should follow it. The amount of deference a court gives an authority is known as the weight of authority. A source's weight depends on its status as primary or secondary, binding or nonbinding. Case law from a higher court in the same jurisdiction is binding or mandatory authority, meaning the court must follow it if presented with similar facts and legal issues. Any source that is not primary is secondary and can only be persuasive to the court, not binding. However, a source can also be primary but not binding/mandatory. For example, a primary persuasive source would be a statute from another state that is not the state where the court decision is being litigated. It is primary because it is a law, but persuasive rather than binding because it is only controlling in another state or jurisdiction.

TYPES OF PRIMARY SOURCES

Constitutions

The supreme law of the land consisting of a set of rules that govern the fundamental rights of a nation or state. It outlines government responsibilities and individual rights. In the United States, we have the U.S. Constitution and individual state constitutions. Constitutions are only applicable when there is state action, meaning the government is taking action or directing a private party to act in a way that may infringe on individual rights.

Statutes

Statues are written laws created by state or federal legislative bodies. Legislature is made up of the Senate and House of Representatives, collectively known as Congress. These rules made by Congress are often referred to as statutory law.

Case Law

Case laws are law based on judicial decisions concerning specific disputes that are heard and resolved by courts. These are laws created by the courts. They are often referred to as common law.

Treaties

Treaties are binding agreements between nations or states that become law. A treaty may not include the word "treaty" in its title but may be called a convention, a pact, a protocol, an accord, or an agreement. For example, the Biological Weapons Convention, the Geneva Protocol, and the Good Friday Agreement are all treaties.

Administrative Rules and Regulations

These are rules created by federal, state, and local agencies that govern policies in a specific area. For example, the local liquor control board may be responsible for issuing licenses or permits in that area. At the federal level, agencies such as the Social Security Administration or the United States Board of Immigration Services make policy for their respective areas. At the state level, the Department of Motor Vehicles makes rules for issuing driver's licenses and other policies related to operating a motor vehicle.

Court Rules

Court rules govern the conduct of business in a particular court. They are procedures adopted by courts that parties and their lawyers must follow on matters within that court's jurisdiction. Every jurisdiction has its own procedures, also known as "local rules." These rules control things like the timeframe to file court documents or meet and confer with opposing parties.

HOW IT WORKS

Some authorities, like those listed above, are primary authorities. Anything other than primary authority is considered secondary authority. The way authority influences the court is called the weight of authority, as mentioned above.

Primary sources do not control the legal questions the court answers unless they are binding on the court. Binding sources are cases from a higher court within that jurisdiction or from prior published cases from the same appellate court. That means, if you are in trial court, a case from an appellate court in the same jurisdiction would be binding on the lower trial court and the judges there would have to follow it. These cases are also called mandatory authority. But a case from an appellate court in a different jurisdiction would not be binding on the trial court. So all cases are primary authority, but not all cases are mandatory. The binding status depends on the jurisdiction and the level of the court issuing the opinion.

When a case is nonbinding, that does not mean it can't be cited. It only means it is not mandatory for the court to follow it. However, a court may find it persuasive, so you may still want to cite it. Persuasive authority can be a secondary source or a primary nonbinding source. These sources may influence the court but not bind it. Only use persuasive authority when there is no primary mandatory authority on your issue or if there is a gap in the law. For example, if there is a self-driving food delivery robot that harms someone in a state, there may not be case law in that state because of the novelty of the delivery system. So the court would look to cases in another state that have had the delivery robots or similar technology longer. Although that other state's case is not binding, it could be persuasive to the court because it is an issue of first impression in its state. Once the novel issue is decided, the state now has precedent for future similar situations that may follow.

Binding case law comes when a lower court appeals to a higher court. If a party does not agree with the decision of the lower court on a legal basis, they have at least one appeal they can make as of right, meaning there is an automatic right to appeal, and the court must hear it. Any other appeal is in the court's discretion to allow. Appeals are usually based on an error in the trial or procedures, or an error in the judge's interpretation of the law. When the appellate court reviews the decision, it can deny the appeal, affirm the appeal, or reverse the appeal. When an appeal is denied or dismissed, the lower court's decision stands. If it is affirmed, the appellate court has overruled the previous decision. If it is reversed, that means it is remanded or sent back to the lower court for a new trial or a modification of the decision. The lower court must reconsider its decision in light of the higher court's decision and correct its previous judgment to be consistent with the appellate decision or have a new trial.

RESEARCHING AND CITING CASES

Case law is the most common primary source used in legal memoranda and pleadings. Cases are a court's written decisions that are collected and published. The collection of cases in each geographic area are printed chronologically in books called reporters. But of course, cases are now available online first. Although that is true, lawyers still cite cases according to their reporter number and page.

Some cases are not published. These unpublished or "nonprecedential" cases may still appear online, but they were not designated to be published in print reporters and should therefore not be cited unless the professor or court rule allows. Some cases are unpublished because they are so new that they simply have not been published in the physical reporter yet. Others are unpublished because the court decided not to publish them due to a lack of precedential value. That cures the problem of having too many written opinions that offer little or nothing new to the law. There are state reporters for state cases and federal reporters for federal cases.

The easiest way to find a case online is if you already have been given a case citation from the professor or supervising attorney. Type the citation in a legal research engine search bar to go directly to the case. Within that case, other opinions will be cited that may be useful for research in the same area. If you do not have a case to start with, you will have to begin researching by typing in a subject, search term, or party name. For example, if you were asked about how to establish guardianship in your state but did not have a case on it, you might search for the word "guardianship" or the term "guardianship over person." Type in a party name if you know there is a case or likely a case involving guardianship and a certain party. If you know the jurisdiction, you can filter your search to a certain state or federal jurisdiction before typing in a search term. In Westlaw and Lexis, you can do a plain language search to find cases that apply to your situation. Click on "Search Tips" to the far right of the search bar in Westlaw for help coming up with synonyms for search terms and connectors to enhance your search. These research engines use artificial intelligence and attorneys to read through each case and pull out the most important legal issues. They can be summarized in the synopsis at the top of the cases. The main legal points will also be listed and summarized in what Westlaw calls headnotes. A key number system is also used to connect headnotes that discuss similar legal issues. It is like using a hashtag in a legal research engine (Figure 2.1). Key numbers in Westlaw classify and organize cases by topic. They help narrow the search to find relevant case law.

One way to find a specific legal issue with key numbers is to search "key numbers" in the Westlaw search bar. Click on the West Key Number System entry in the popup window. Choose the topic of interest. Then, click "View Headnotes" at the top or click on the link of the chosen topic. From there, you can narrow by jurisdiction and view various key numbers for a more specific search. Searching headnotes related to your topic provides a broader option. Finding specific key numbers provides a narrower search option. Headnotes are always listed at the top of cases on Westlaw. They are a good way to enter the key number system and get the answer you are looking for faster. Finding one on-point case, a case with similar facts and issues, can lead to others through the key number system.

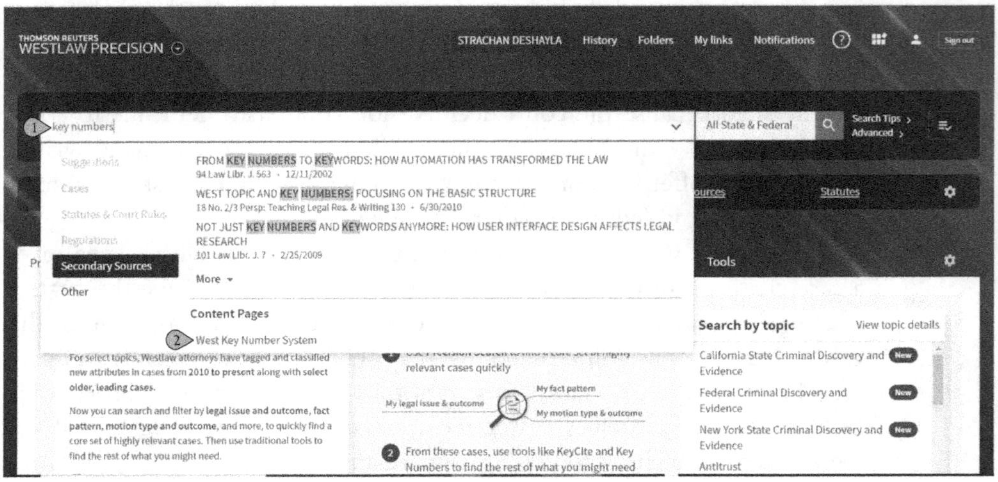

1 Key numbers

2 West key number system

Figure 2.1 Finding a Case with Key Numbers

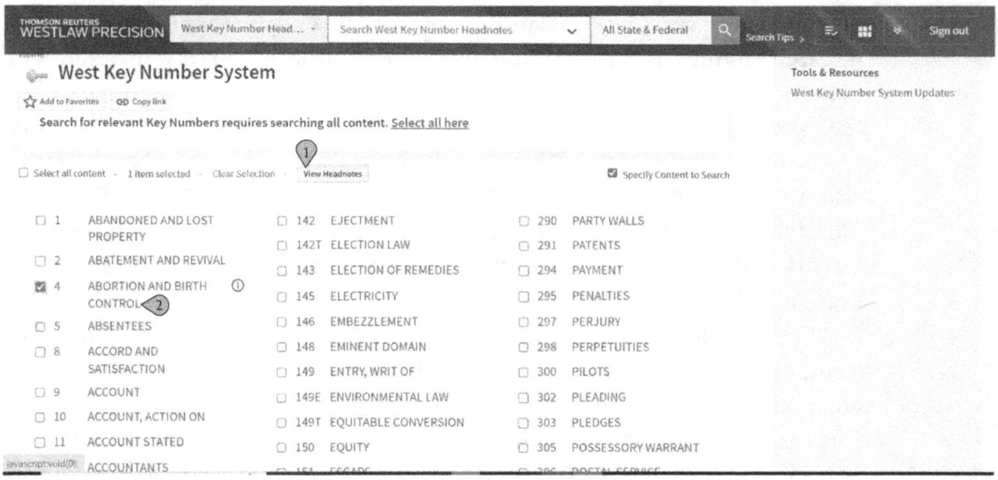

1 View headnotes

2 Abortion and birth control

Figure 2.2 Viewing Headnotes

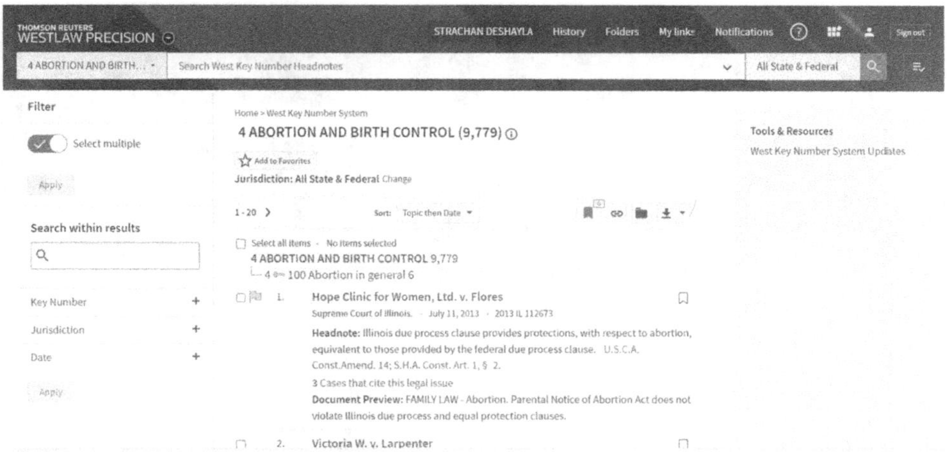

Figure 2.3 Results After Clicking "View Headnotes"

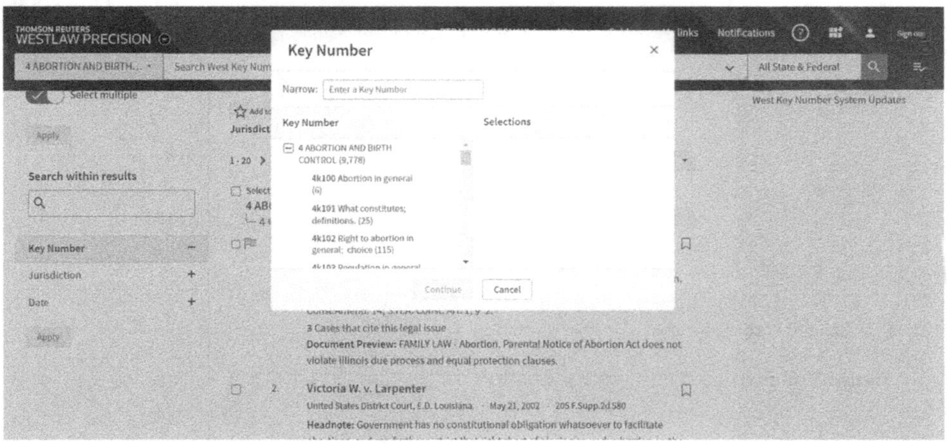

Figure 2.4 Choose a Key Number

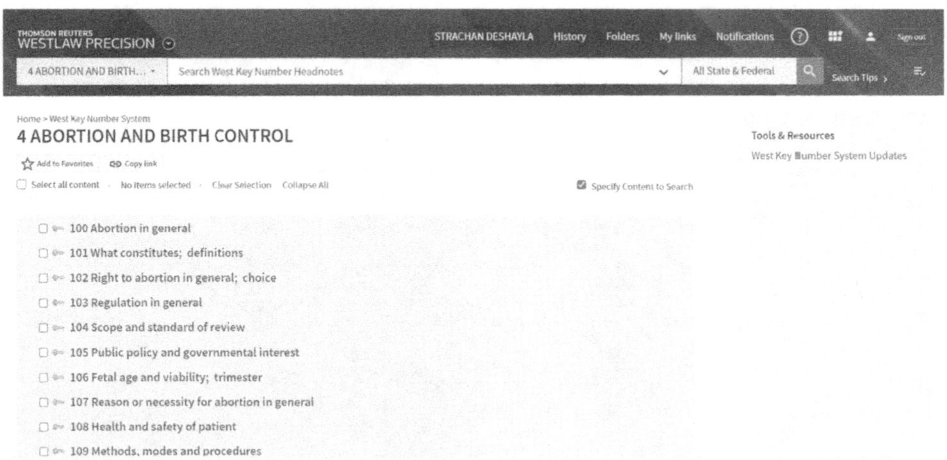

Figure 2.5 Results After Clicking on Topic

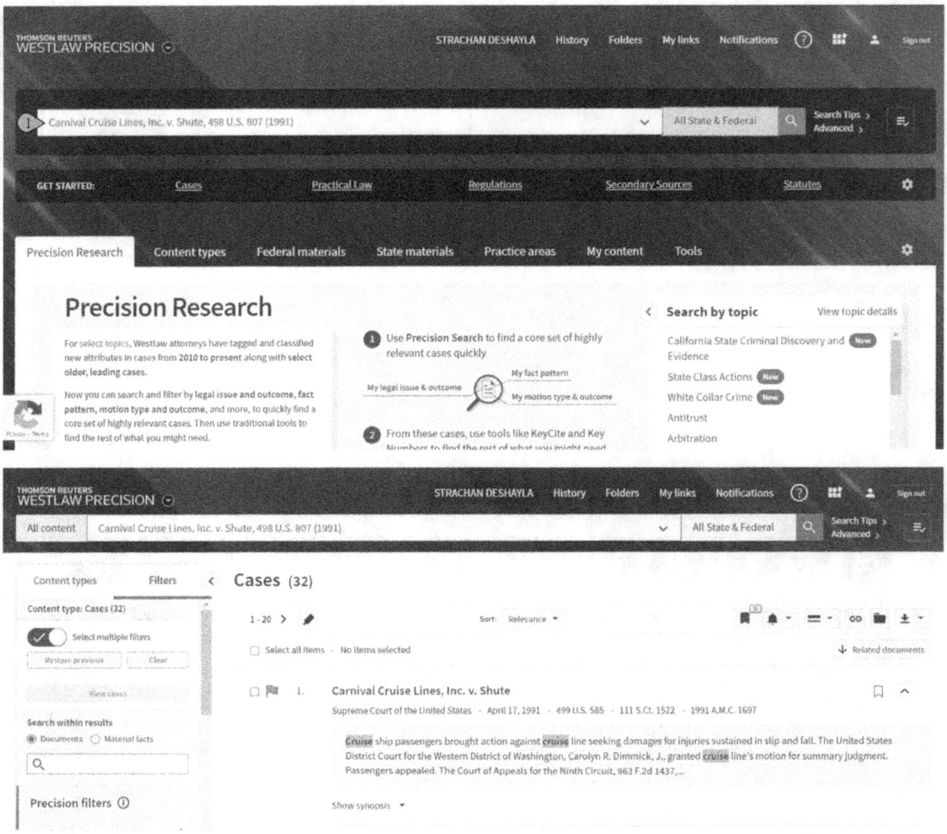

1 *Carnival* case citation

Figure 2.6 Finding a Case with a Citation

1 Synopsis

Figure 2.7 Synopsis

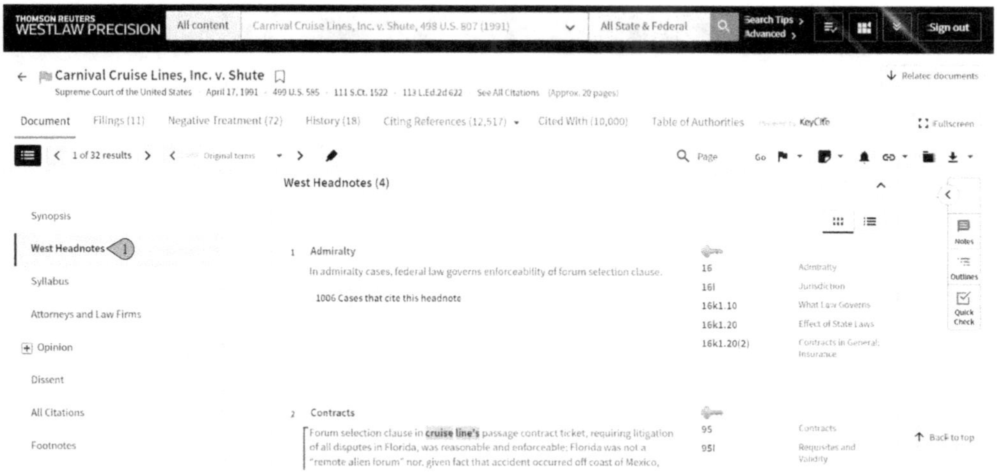

1 West headnotes

Figure 2.8 West Headnotes

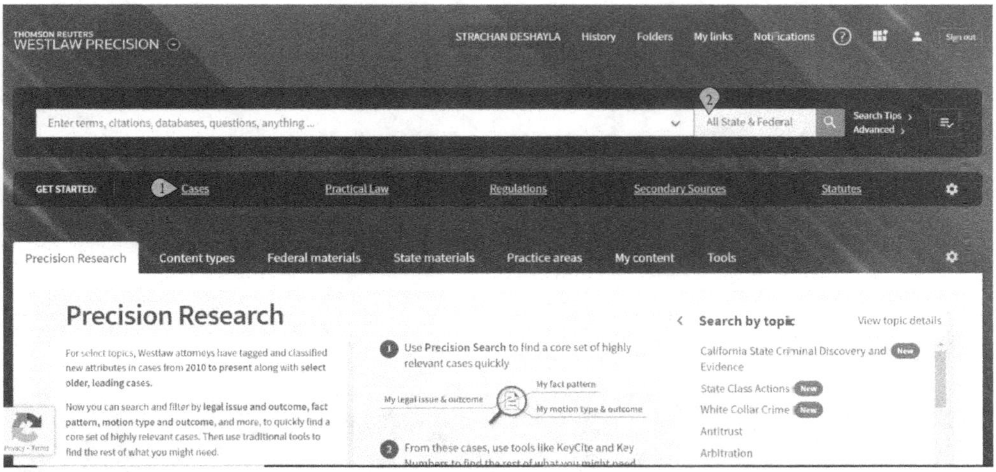

1 Cases

2 All state & federal

Figure 2.9 Finding a Case by Filtering

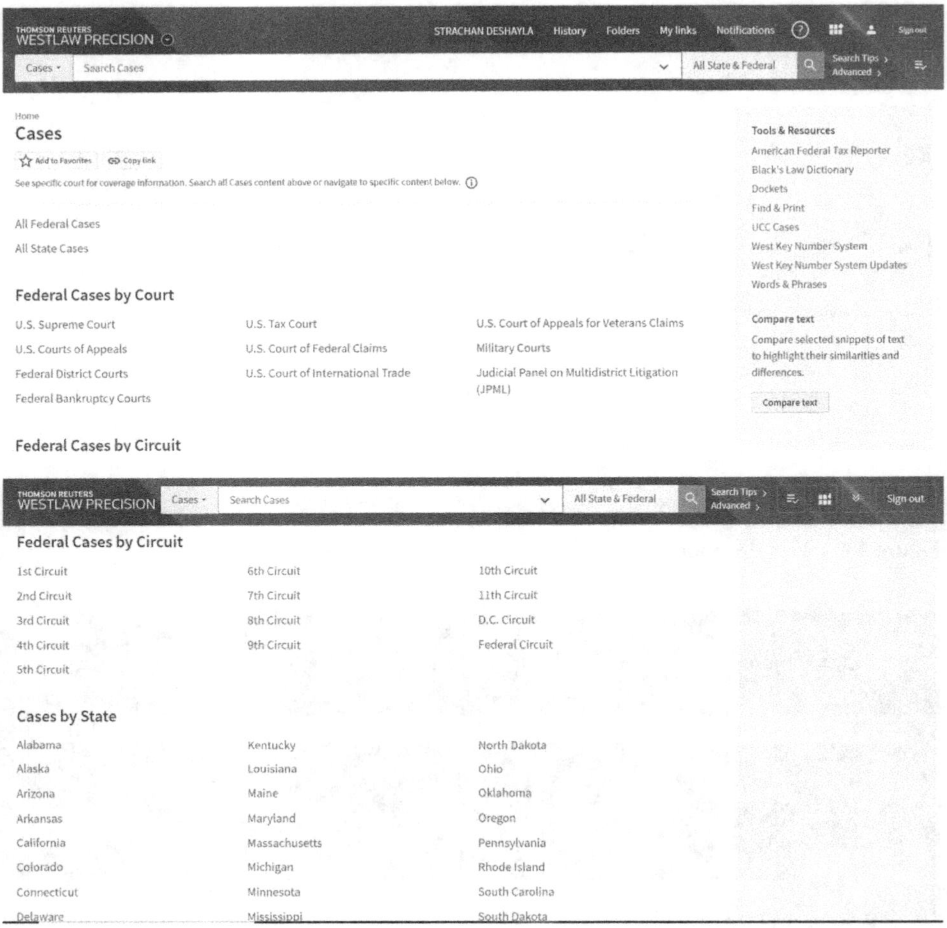

Figure 2.10 Choose Federal, State, or Court

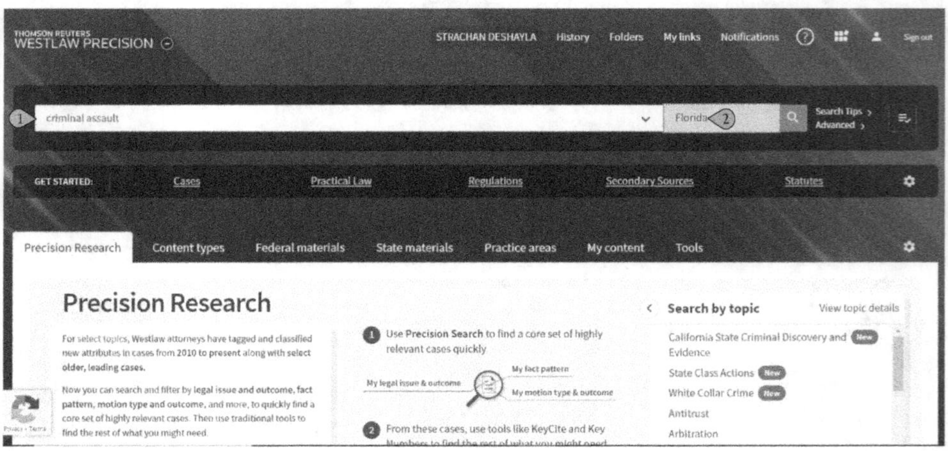

① Search bar

② Florida

Figure 2.11 Finding a Case with Search Term

Choose cases or use precision filters (Figure 2.12) on the left panel. Precision filters are Westlaw's advanced filters that give a researcher more options to narrow search results.

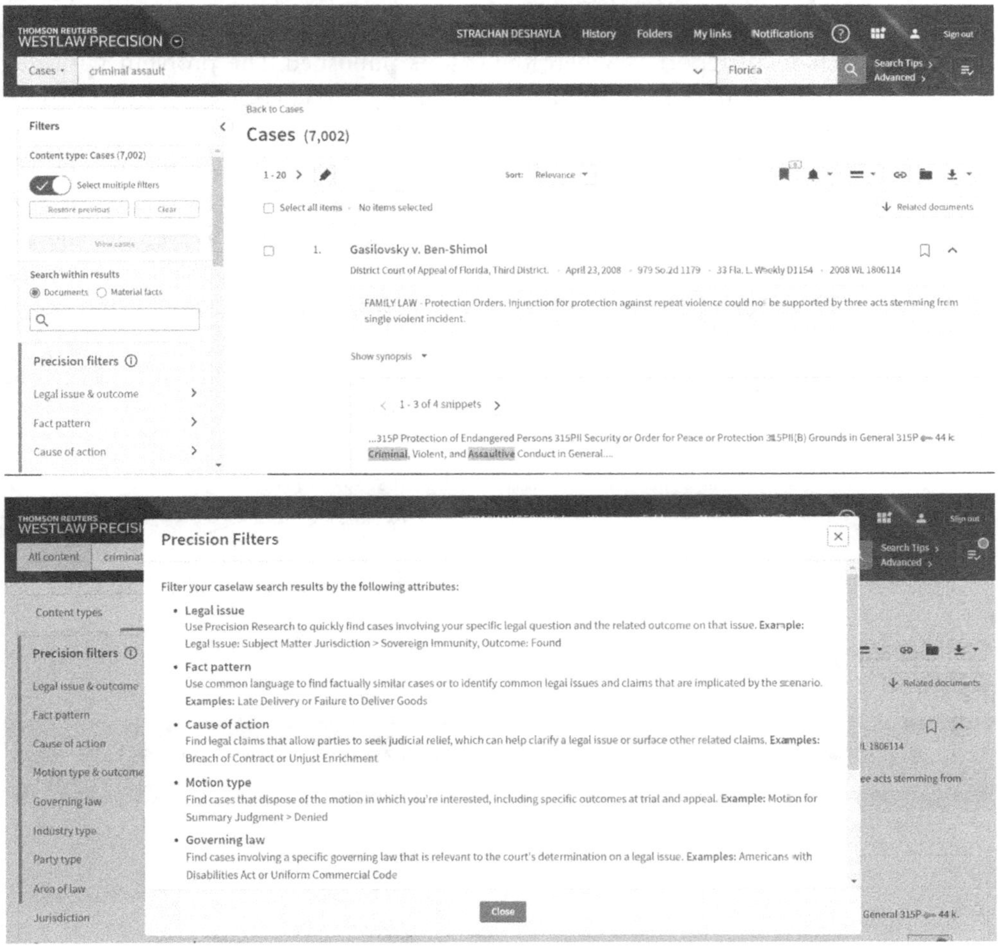

Figure 2.12 Precision Filters

CASE CITATIONS

Legal research engines such as Westlaw will list each reporter where the case is published, but they do not provide correct citations to a case. As a researcher, you researcher must find which reporter to cite to and the proper citation form. To do that, you must use a citation guide such as the Bluebook, ALWD Citation Guide, or a citation manual published by your state. There is an online version of the Bluebook but it does not have a citation generator. It is used in the same way as a physical copy. There may be online citation generators available for a fee. However, it is best to write your own citations so you can ensure accuracy.

It may be tempting to choose to "copy citation" in Westlaw but that will not produce a proper Bluebook citation. The Westlaw citation will include all reporters where the case is published. The problem with that is that in most law schools and in many jurisdictions, parallel citations (citing multiple reporters) is not proper citation form. Generally, only one reporter should be cited. The Westlaw citation will also not include the pincite to the exact page where the statement of law is located. It may not include the correct abbreviations for certain words as well. To find the correct reporter to cite and the correct abbreviations, use Table T1 near the back of the Bluebook. Below is the citation formed when clicking "copy citation" in Westlaw.

Carnival Cruise Lines, Inc. v. Shute, 499 U.S. 585, 111 S. Ct. 1522, 113 L. Ed. 2d 622 (1991)

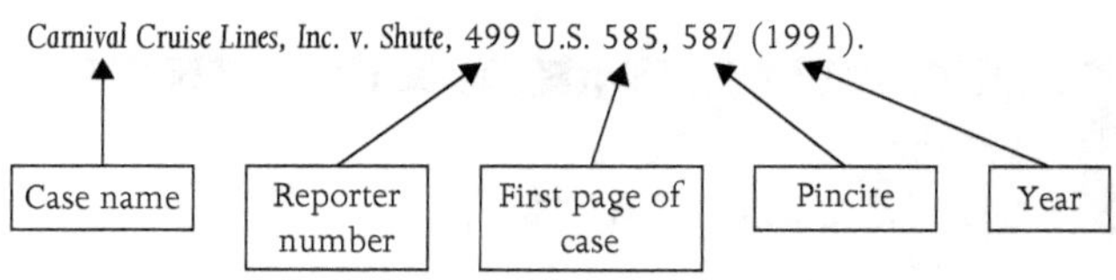

Figure 2.13 Proper Bluebook Citation

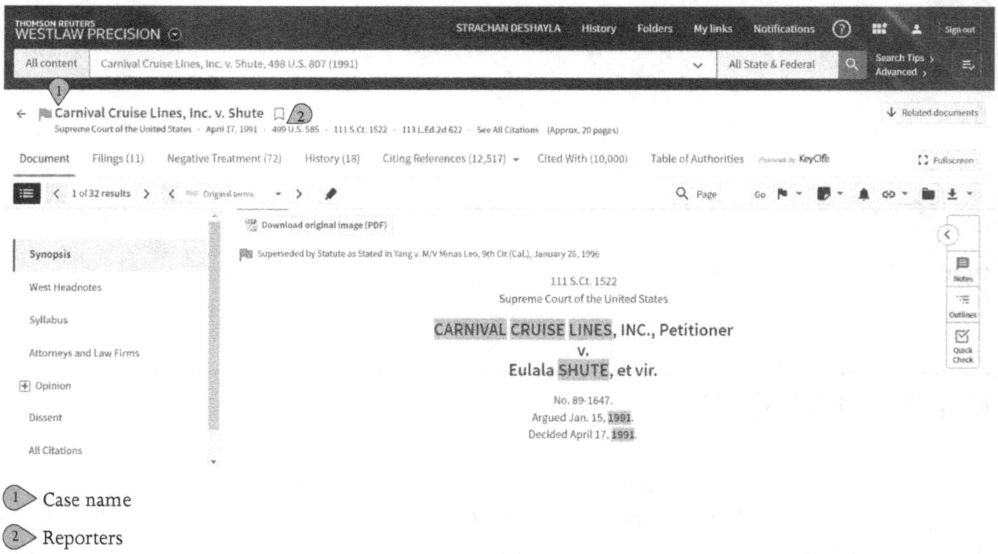

Figure 2.14 Case Name in Westlaw Precision

Figure 2.15 Proper Full Case Citation

Within legal documents, often after the first full citation has been used, a short citation is then used as an abridged version, typically only including the case name and relevant page number. This allows for streamlined references within the same discussion. Note that a short case name must always be in italics or underlined so that everyone knows that the case itself is being referenced rather than the actual plaintiff or defendant from the case.

Short cite to same case:

Carnival Cruise Lines, 499 U.S. at 587.

Shortest short cite to same case immediately preceding and on the same page:

Id.

Shortest short cite to case immediately preceding but on a different page:

Id. at 587.

EVALUATING AND EFFECTIVELY CITING CASES

During your research you will find many, many cases. When citing case law, it is best to stick to published decisions. Whether a case is published or not is usually stated at the top of a legal research engine. After sorting your options according to authority, review each relevant case by reading them critically to see how the court held on each issue. A case's holding is the decision the court made. The holding can also be described as the answer to the legal question presented. Use citator tools on Westlaw and Lexis to determine if the case is still good law on your issue. More on that later in Chapter 7. Once an on-point case is found, in your own words, come up with the rule of law from the case. Write it down and cite the case after each sentence of the rule or explanation of the law. Once you have fully cited a case for the first time in a document, use a short cite for that case from then on.

Use cases to explain the law. Case law tells attorneys how a court treated or interpreted a statute or a certain factual scenario. It also demonstrates how courts may rule in a similar case. So, the best way to explain the law is by explaining and summarizing the rules of case law. Compare your client's facts to the facts of a similar case that held the way you want the court to rule on your issue. Comparisons or analogical reasoning make the cases cited even more clear and persuasive. When a particular case or cases are cited often within the sources found in your research, those are likely the leading cases on an issue. Be sure to analyze the leading cases to make sure your research is comprehensive.

For Educational Use Only

Dobbs v. Jackson Women's Health Organization, 597 U.S. 215 (2022)

142 S.Ct. 2228, 213 L.Ed.2d 545, Med & Med GD (CCH) P 307,405...

KeyCite Yellow Flag - Negative Treatment

Not Followed as Dicta State v. Gantt, Wash.App. Div. 1, January 2, 2024

(1) 142 S.Ct. 2228

(2) Supreme Court of the United States.

Thomas E. DOBBS, State Health Officer of the Mississippi Department of Health, et al., Petitioners

v.

JACKSON WOMEN'S HEALTH ORGANIZATION, et al.

(3) No. 19-1392

|

Argued December 1, 2021

|

Decided June 24, 2022

Synopsis (4)

Background: Sole facility providing abortion services in Mississippi, as well as one of its abortion providers, brought action against state officials responsible for overseeing health care and medical licensing, challenging constitutionality of Mississippi's Gestational Age Act which prohibited abortions after 15 weeks' gestation except in medical emergency or in case of severe fetal abnormality. The United States District Court for the Southern District of Mississippi, Carlton Reeves, J., 349 F.Supp.3d 536, granted facility's motion to limit discovery to the issue of viability, granted plaintiffs' summary judgment motion, and permanently enjoined the Act in all applications. Defendants appealed. The United States Court of Appeals for the Fifth Circuit, Higginbotham, Senior Circuit Judge, 945 F.3d 265, affirmed. Certiorari was granted.

(5)

Holdings: The Supreme Court, Justice Alito, held that:

[1] federal constitution does not provide a right to abortion, and authority to regulate abortion must be returned to the people and their elected representatives, overruling *Roe v. Wade*, 410 U.S. 113, 93 S.Ct. 705, 35 L.Ed.2d 147, and *Planned Parenthood of Southeastern Pennsylvania v. Casey*, 505 U.S. 833, 112 S.Ct. 2791, 120 L.Ed.2d 674, and abrogating *Doe v. Bolton*, 410 U.S. 179, 93 S.Ct. 739, 35 L.Ed.2d 201, *Colautti v. Franklin*, 439 U.S. 379, 99 S.Ct. 675, 58 L.Ed.2d 596, *Whole Woman's Health v. Hellerstedt*, 579 U.S. 582, 136 S.Ct. 2292, 195 L.Ed.2d 665, *June Medical Services L.L.C. v. Russo*, 140 S.Ct. 2103, 207 L.Ed.2d 566, and other cases, and

[2] on rational-basis review for constitutional violation, legitimate interests supported Mississippi's Gestational Age Act.

Reversed and remanded.

Justice Thomas filed a concurring opinion.

Justice Kavanaugh filed a concurring opinion.

Chief Justice Roberts filed an opinion concurring in the judgment.

Justices Breyer, Sotomayor, and Kagan filed a dissenting opinion.

Procedural Posture(s): Petition for Writ of Certiorari; On Appeal; Motion for Permanent Injunction; Motion for Summary Judgment.

West Headnotes (36) (6)

[1] **Abortion and Birth Control** Right to abortion in general; choice

Constitutional Law Abortion, Contraception, and Birth Control

The Constitution makes no reference to abortion and no such right is implicitly protected by any constitutional provision, including substantive due process principles under the Due Process Clause of the Fourteenth Amendment, which Clause has been held to guarantee some substantive rights that are not mentioned in the Constitution if they are deeply rooted in the Nation's history and tradition and implicit in the concept of ordered liberty, a category in which a right to abortion, which involves the destruction of fetal life, does not fall, and thus, the

WESTLAW © 2024 Thomson Reuters. No claim to original U.S. Government Works. 1

(1) Reporter (3) Volume number (5) Holdings

(2) Case name (4) Synopsis (6) Headnotes

Figure 2.16 Anatomy of a Case

19 Cases that cite this headnote

[36] **Abortion and Birth Control** ⇐ Fetal age and viability; trimester

Abortion and Birth Control ⇐ Health and safety of patient

Abortion and Birth Control ⇐ Methods, modes and procedures

On rational-basis review for constitutional violation, legitimate interests supported Mississippi's Gestational Age Act, which prohibited abortions after 15 weeks' gestation except in medical emergency or in case of severe fetal abnormality; Mississippi legislature's findings recounted the stages of human prenatal development and asserted State's interest in protecting the life of the unborn, legislature also found that abortions performed after 15 weeks typically used dilation and evacuation procedure, and legislature found the use of that procedure for nontherapeutic or elective reasons to be a barbaric practice, dangerous for the maternal patient, and demeaning to the medical profession. Miss. Code Ann. § 41-41-191(2)(b)(i), (4)(b).

8 Cases that cite this headnote

West Codenotes

Negative Treatment Reconsidered
Miss. Code Ann. § 41-41-191

****2234** *Syllabus* [*] (1)

***215** Mississippi's Gestational Age Act provides that "[e]xcept in a medical emergency or in the case of a severe fetal abnormality, a person shall not intentionally or knowingly perform ... or induce an abortion of an unborn human being if the probable gestational age of the unborn human being has been determined to be greater than fifteen (15) weeks." Miss. Code Ann. § 41–41–191. Respondents—Jackson Women's Health Organization, an abortion clinic, and one of its doctors—challenged the Act in Federal District Court, alleging that it violated this Court's precedents establishing a constitutional right to abortion, in particular *Roe v. Wade*, 410 U.S. 113, 93 S.Ct. 705, 35 L.Ed.2d 147, and *Planned Parenthood of Southeastern Pa. v. Casey*, 505 U.S. 833, 112 S.Ct. 2791, 120 L.Ed.2d 674. The District Court granted summary judgment in favor of respondents and permanently enjoined enforcement of the Act, reasoning that Mississippi's 15-week restriction on abortion violates this Court's cases forbidding States to ban abortion pre-viability. The Fifth Circuit affirmed. Before this Court, petitioners defend the Act on the grounds that *Roe* and *Casey* were wrongly decided and that the Act is constitutional because it satisfies rational-basis review.

Held: The Constitution does not confer a right to abortion; (2) *Roe* and *Casey* are overruled; and the authority to regulate abortion is returned to the people and their elected representatives. Pp. 2244 – 2285.

(a) The critical question is whether the Constitution, properly understood, confers a right to obtain an abortion. *Casey*'s controlling opinion skipped over that question and reaffirmed *Roe* solely on the basis of *stare decisis*. A proper application of *stare decisis*, however, requires an assessment of the strength of the grounds on which *Roe* was based. The Court therefore turns to the question that the *Casey* plurality did not consider. Pp. 2244 – 2258.

(1) First, the Court reviews the standard that the Court's cases have used to determine whether the Fourteenth Amendment's reference to "liberty" protects ****2235** a particular right. The Constitution makes no express reference to a right to obtain an abortion, but several constitutional provisions have been offered as potential homes for an implicit constitutional right. *Roe* held that the abortion right is part of a right ***216** to privacy that springs from the First, Fourth, Fifth, Ninth, and Fourteenth Amendments. See 410 U.S. at 152–153, 93 S.Ct. 705. The *Casey* Court grounded its decision solely on the theory that the right to obtain an abortion is part of the "liberty" protected by the Fourteenth Amendment's Due Process Clause. Others have suggested that support can be found in the Fourteenth Amendment's Equal Protection Clause, but that theory is squarely foreclosed by the Court's precedents, which establish that a State's regulation of abortion is not a sex-based classification and is thus not subject to the heightened scrutiny that applies to such

(1) Syllabus

(2) Holding

Figure 2.16 Continued

Examples

1. In a Florida trial court, you are arguing against a summary judgment motion filed by the defense. Opposing counsel submits a case that has similar facts and holds for the defendant. It is a California trial court case. What is your best argument to discredit this case?
   a. It does not have the exact same facts. A case must be on point or else it does not apply.
   b. The case is from a lower or equal court, and it is outside of your jurisdiction, so it is not binding on this court.
   c. Florida courts can never rely on California cases.
   d. This case is secondary authority.

2. During a legal research class, the professor asks you to use only primary authority in the upcoming memo assignment. Which of the following can be used?
   a. The Restatement of Torts
   b. *Smith v. Consuelo*, 923 S. 2d 161 (Ga. 2002)
   c. Fla. Stat. 92.60
   d. Both b and c

3. The appellate court in the Sixth Circuit of Texas hears cases from 19 counties. One of the counties in its jurisdiction had a case overturned by the court. What must the lower court in that county do now?
   a. Follow the appellate court ruling and modify its decision to be consistent with the Sixth Circuit ruling.
   b. Consider the appellate court ruling but do what it wants anyway.
   c. Decline to follow the higher court because its decision comes clothed with the presumption of correctness.
   d. Keep its order the same regardless of the Sixth Circuit discussion.

4. In legal research class, the professor tells you some facts about a woman who was threatened and nearly punched in Louisiana. She asks you to find a primary source that provides what the state law for assault is in that state. You happen to know that in some states an assault does not have to involve a touching. What is the best way to find the common law in Louisiana?
   a. Find an article online about Louisiana law.
   b. Look for state statutes that define the criminal code.
   c. Search for cases in Louisiana on a legal research engine that discuss and define criminal assault.
   d. Ask common people who live in the state to tell you the law.

5. You are a certified legal intern at the state prosecutor's office. In court, you hear opposing counsel cite and discuss an article about DUI breathalyzer results from a well-respected local newspaper. At a court recess,

your supervising attorney asks you to review the article and come up with an argument against it. What do you do?

a. Skip the article and argue that nobody reads newspapers anymore.
b. Review the article and then review binding case law in the jurisdiction that contradicts it. Argue the binding primary source trumps the article, which is a persuasive source.
c. Read the article and agree that it makes a valid point.
d. Find more articles from better newspapers to combat their article.

6. While researching for a memorandum in support of the motion for summary judgment in your legal research class, you are having a hard time finding cases on malfunctioning electric bicycles in California. There are a couple of good, on-point cases in New York and Florida. Are these cases acceptable to include?
   a. Yes, if there are no on-point cases in California.
   b. Yes, because New York and Florida are great vacation destinations.
   c. No. Only California cases can be used because the incident happened there.
   d. No. Courts in California do not like East Coast court decisions.

7. After doing hours of research, you find an on-point case outside of the jurisdiction and a similar binding case within the jurisdiction that supports your argument but is easily distinguished. Which case should you use?
   a. Apply the shortest case so it's faster to read.
   b. Use the out-of-state case only because it is the same exact situation.
   c. Both.
   d. Neither case. It's too hard to decide.

Explanations

1. (a.) Incorrect. Of course, it is great when a case has the same exact facts as your client's case, but that is not required for a case to apply. Similar facts or other case facts can be compared to your client's case to make the case applicable, but it must still be in a higher court in the same jurisdiction to be binding. But keep in mind that prior published appellate court cases are binding on subsequent appellate court cases. **(b.) Correct.** Cases from a lower court are not binding on a higher court. Further, cases from outside of the jurisdiction are also not binding. Here, we have a case that is both from a lower or equal level court and it is outside of the Florida jurisdiction. So, it is not binding on the court. That is the best argument from these answer choices to discredit opposing counsel's case. (c.) Incorrect. Just because a case is from outside of the jurisdiction does not mean an attorney cannot rely on it and a court therefore follow it. However, it can only be relied on as persuasive authority if there is a gap

in the law in your jurisdiction. Then, a court may decide to follow it or decline to follow it. (d.) Incorrect. Cases are primary authority because they are actual legal rules made by the court. But not all cases are binding or controlling on every court. For a case to control a court's decision, it would need to be in a higher court in the same jurisdiction. Even though the case is from outside of the jurisdiction, it is still primary authority.

2. (a.) Incorrect. The Restatement of Torts is a treatise that summarizes the law. It is not a court case or other law. Therefore, it is a secondary source. **(d.) Correct.** Both (b.) and (c.) are correct. The *Smith v. Consuelo* case and the Florida statute are both primary sources that could control a court's decision. They are rules, state legislation, or court-made law.

3. **(a.) Correct.** The trial court must follow the higher court decision when it determines there was an error. In the appellate opinion, the court will likely state that it is sending the case back down or remanding it for a ruling consistent with its decision. (b.) Incorrect. The trial court is not permitted to ignore the appellate court's ruling because the appellate court is a higher court. (c.) Incorrect. The trial court does not have discretion to decline to follow a higher court's ruling in its same jurisdiction. It may decline to follow a higher court outside of its jurisdiction, however. (d.) Incorrect. For all the above reasons, this answer is incorrect. The trial court cannot ignore the higher court's ruling when it is inconsistent with its decision. It is also a direct order from the appeals court directly above it.

4. (a.) Incorrect. An article might assist in finding the correct criminal code, but the professor asked for a primary source. The article is a secondary source. Also, the article could be incorrect or outdated. (b.) Incorrect. Statutes will state the criminal law but are often vague or leave gaps. Case law will interpret the statute and fill some gaps. The question also asks for common law, not statutory law. **(c.) Correct.** It is best to use a legal research engine to search for cases that discuss similar facts. It is likely that these cases will mention and interpret the applicable criminal statute. (d.) Incorrect. Lay people may not know the exact criminal code. Common law does not mean asking common people!

5. (a.) Incorrect. As an intern or attorney, it is important to do what a supervising attorney reasonably asks. Even if news articles are not the main source of news or law anymore, there may be points of discussion involved that have been settled by actual laws, also known as primary authority. It could also be an opinion piece or article that is not exactly on point with the issue at hand. **(b.) Correct.** This is the best answer. Read the article to see what point was made that motivated opposing counsel to share it in court. Find case law that contradicts the comments in the article or distinguishes it from your facts. Argue that the article

does not apply because there is binding case law that says otherwise and that the factual scenario is different anyway. (c.) Incorrect. While agreeing with the other side is reasonable on minor issues, it is not the direction you were given. You were asked to make an argument against it. Even if valid points are made, it can be argued that it is persuasive authority when primary authority is available. (d.) Incorrect. Finding more articles that contradict the article could be helpful, but it is best to find primary authority.

6. **(a.) Correct.** Cases outside of the jurisdiction may be persuasive to the California court if there are no similar cases on the issue in its own jurisdiction. The New York and Florida cases would be considered persuasive primary authority. They are persuasive because they are from a different jurisdiction and the court does not have to follow them. They are primary because they are case law, which are court-made laws and not an article or other commentary on the law. Be sure to explain why you are relying on it and how it applies to your case facts. (b.) Incorrect. The reputations of the states are irrelevant. (c.) Incorrect. Again, the reputation of the state is not the point. Out-of-state cases can still be used to support your argument. (d.) Incorrect. Cases from other states, while not binding, always have the potential to be persuasive.

7. (a.) Incorrect. The length of the court decision should not be a factor in deciding which cases to cite. (b.) While it is tempting to use only cases that are exactly like your client's facts, binding cases should be cited first because the court must follow them. **(c.) Correct.** This is the best answer. Both cases could be cited. Cite the binding case first and cite the persuasive case next to further support your argument. (d.) Incorrect. When in doubt, cite both. Do not give up and move on to other cases. At the very least, they should both be saved to reevaluate later.

CHAPTER 3

Law Gathering: Secondary Sources

SECONDARY SOURCES

What is a secondary source? First things first. Second things second.

Secondary sources are texts related to the law that are not law. They have not been codified because they have not been created by courts or legislative bodies. They explain, analyze, critique, or comment on the law but do not create or establish law. One popular collection of secondary sources you may have heard of is the *American Law Reports*, which contains articles written by practicing attorneys. Your school's law review and law journals are also common secondary sources. These student-led journals contain articles and essays from law students, law professors, and attorneys.

When researching online, it's important to know which sources are primary sources and which are secondary sources. Although secondary sources are not law or binding on any court, they can be quite persuasive when there is little or no law on a particular issue in the jurisdiction. They are important to the legal researcher because they explain the law and often contain useful primary sources.

For example, if a law is fairly new, there likely will not be many, if any, cases regarding the issue that the law affects. So, when there is no case to start with, a law review article about the new law may be helpful to learn about the law and likely will cite other similar articles. It will likely cite relevant cases as well. Then, you have cases or other primary sources to continue your research.

Think of a secondary source like advice from a trusted friend or colleague. It may be persuasive. It's something to think about, but you don't have to follow it. That is how the court looks at secondary sources. Courts may find that these sources are influential, but they are not bound by them. Certain secondary sources may be more persuasive than others. A restatement of the law authored by a well-known and respected judge or law professor may be more influential than a law journal article written by a law student, for example. These types of sources are a great place to start your legal research if you do not have a primary source to jump start your research. When there is no known law to start from, a secondary source about the legal issue could definitely help get things going.

When to Use Secondary Sources

Secondary sources are used when there is no legal precedent or if you are unfamiliar with a topic. For example, when changing practice areas or being presented with a unique legal question, the law area or question is unfamiliar and reading up on the topic can assist you at the beginning of your research. Secondary sources may also be helpful when an overwhelming amount of legal material is found. They will help the researcher learn about a particular topic so they can perform a more informed search. And as mentioned, secondary sources can also be used to find primary sources. Primary sources found within secondary sources should be verified and updated before relying on them in your own research.

Courts will consider secondary sources in the same way. When a court seeks the prevailing view on how primary sources interpret the law in a certain area, it may review a secondary source. That is because sources like law articles and restatements may show the consensus among legal scholars and practitioners and aid in the court's decision when there is a lack of precedent in its jurisdiction. They often include leading cases that have settled a point of law that can aid the researcher in her quest.

Citing secondary sources is not recommended if there are proper primary sources. But, if you must, restatements and treatises are often viewed more favorably by courts over other secondary sources. Restatements of law contain statements of common law rules and often become law if a jurisdiction adopts them as law or a court cites favorably to them in an opinion. Treatises tend to focus on a specific practice area and can be scholarly or geared toward practitioners, so they are among the most trusted secondary sources due to their depth and wide acceptance. But generally, approach secondary sources carefully in your research. Be cognizant of the date the source was written. Consider if the law has changed since the source was written. Typically, practical publications written by attorneys are more practice focused and may be updated more often than other pieces written by legal scholars who have a more theoretical approach to the law.

TYPES OF SECONDARY SOURCES

Common legal secondary sources include the following:

Legal Dictionaries

Knowing what the words mean is half the battle. Legal dictionaries help explain unfamiliar legal lingo. Understanding unknown words will help build knowledge on the research topic.

Law Journals and Law Review Articles

Law journals and law review articles are helpful for providing background information on a topic. They are written by law students, law professors, attorneys, judges, and other legal professionals. The authors of these articles are making their own arguments and giving opinions. These pieces contain many footnotes that support their statements. Footnotes may provide other secondary sources or primary sources that may be useful to your research.

Restatements

Restatements of the law cover basic doctrines governing American law. They are written by leading scholars in their respective fields. They are highly regarded by courts. Restatements are a national resource that provide an overview of legal principles like torts, property, contracts, etc. They are not updated regularly and may go years without a new edition.

Legal Encyclopedias

Legal encyclopedias can be national or state sources. They are organized by topic and are a great introduction to a subject. They give background or a general overview of a topic. *American Jurisprudence* is a popular national encyclopedia. Many states have their own legal encyclopedia, which is ideal for researching that state's laws.

Treatises

Treatises are similar to legal encyclopedias except they are organized by the area of law. They have a narrower focus, providing more detail and insight.

These sources are also often written in a more scholarly tone, meaning they can be more formal and academic. Popular legal treatises include *Farnsworth on Contracts* and *Prosser on Torts*. They are updated more frequently than restatements, with updates often coming once or twice a year.

Practice Guides

These state-specific sources are written by attorneys for attorneys. They are practical guides that often include directions, strategies, and authorities. They are straightforward explanations about the state law and are frequently updated.

Jury Instructions

These instructions are a practice-focused secondary source and practice aid. They are helpful to lawyers and judges during the trial process when instructing the jury on the law. They outline the law for laypeople by explaining the basic elements of a legal issue. They can be found online on Westlaw, Lexis, and Bloomberg, as well as state-specific websites. Jury instructions are necessarily much shorter than other secondary sources. They are very narrow due to their purpose of instructing a jury and as such do not contain as much information on the law as compared to other sources.

Amicus Briefs

Known as a "friend-of-the-court" brief, an amicus brief is a legal document submitted by a non-party to a case. The brief offers additional information, arguments, or expertise to help it decide the case. Such a brief may be cited as a secondary source.

Here are some common non-legal secondary sources (note that these sources need greater verification and you should be careful when using them):

Google Scholar

Google Scholar is a free search engine that provides a host of academic literature. Here, one can search for information across many disciplines. You may find books, abstracts, articles, theses, and court opinions. However, the site is limited in its scope and reliability. All sources indexed here may not have been verified.

Blawgs

A blawg is a slang term for an online law journal or blog that focuses primarily on law-related issues. They are usually written by law students, law professors, or lawyers who share insights, advice, and news in a conversational and engaging way.

Wikipedia

Wikipedia is a free online encyclopedia that anyone can edit. The articles provide links to related websites with additional information on the topics searched. It is not a reliable source because it can be edited by anyone at any time and may contain incorrect information.

Books

Books written about law-related issues by authors who may not be legal experts.

News Articles

Non-legal sources also include articles in newspapers or news websites about law-related news written by journalists. These reporters may have no legal background but often quote the opinions of experts in the field.

Generative Artificial Intelligence Engines (e.g., ChatGPT)

Chatbots or AI platforms are large language models that gather information from various web sources. The information is not verified and may not be accurate.

SCHOLARLY RESEARCH

When researching for an essay or scholarly paper, the above legal and non-legal secondary sources can be used, but there are also search engines that are specifically used for legal scholarship. These search engines have large databases of articles and other legal materials. Law students may need to do scholarly research when they are selected for a law review or law journal, or when required to produce upper-level writing before graduation. This type of research differs a bit from other methods of online legal research. In practice, scholarly research will likely only be done if you are writing an article for a law journal or are employed in legal academia where the position requires publications. Most research done as an attorney will instead be in search of primary sources that can be used to predict or persuade the court.

Before doing scholarly research, the researcher must first identify a topic of interest. Then, preliminary research must be done to make sure that the topic is not oversaturated. If too many articles come up, that may mean there is already much written on the topic and the researcher may need to narrow the topic. If the opposite happens and too few articles come up, the topic likely needs to be broadened. Narrow the search terms or use synonyms to find fewer but more relevant articles. Expand the topic in the search terms to find more articles. For example, if searching for "natural disasters," many articles will be produced because of the broad term. But if you search "natural disasters in the Midwest region of the United States" or "tornados, earthquakes, and hurricanes in the United States," fewer articles may populate, but they will be more useful because they are specific to your topic. Once enough research is done, take notes, and begin to write.

Here are some scholarly legal research engines:

HeinOnline (https://home.heinonline.org/)

This internet database houses a large number of legal materials. Its materials include academic law review articles, commercially produced law journals and magazines, reported cases, statutes, regulations, and treatises. This database has millions of pages in an online, searchable, image-based format.

Westlaw

This legal research engine not only has numerous primary sources in its database, but also secondary sources such as many scholarly articles, treatises, legal encyclopedias, ALR Annotations, and the Restatements.

Lexis

In this legal research platform, a researcher can find scholarly articles, treatises, legal encyclopedias, ALR Annotations, and the Restatements within its secondary materials database.

SSRN (https://www.ssrn.com/index.cfm/en/)

The Social Science Research Network is a repository of scholarly research. It is a collection of works in progress, accepted papers, and published papers. Users can view and download articles on this network.

Google Scholar

This free search engine provides a way to broadly search for scholarly material. It has an array of full-text articles, court opinions, and literature. The researcher can download articles but may be charged a fee for the full document. However, see above for the downsides of using Google Scholar.

When deciding which platform to conduct your scholarly research in, consider the reliability of the site. Again, Google Scholar often has sources that have not been verified or are limited in scope. As for the others, because they are traditional academic research sites and have been verified and peer reviewed, they are more reliable platforms.

HOW IT WORKS

Imagine that as a first-year associate in a top law firm, your supervising attorney asks you about the law on an unfamiliar topic. There is no legal precedent. In the legal research engine of your choosing, you click on Secondary Sources (Figure 3.1). Filter to the correct jurisdiction. Filter by the type of publication, such as law journal, treatise, or restatement (Figure 3.2). Type in the question at issue or a search term. Review the applicable sources. Within the secondary source, there is often an option to annotate, save to a folder, download, or print. It is best practice to highlight important information and save the source to a folder for easy finding later.

Primary sources such as cases and statutes found within the secondary source could lead to the answer to the legal problem. So although they are secondary sources in name, these sources are actually where you begin if not given a case or statute to start with, or you are dealing with an unfamiliar area of law. They will give you an overview of the law, offer citations to primary sources to review, and provide you with a more informed search. They can assist with determining the current view of the law and help predict the direction the law is heading. Secondary sources will often clarify for you the leading cases in a particular area of law.

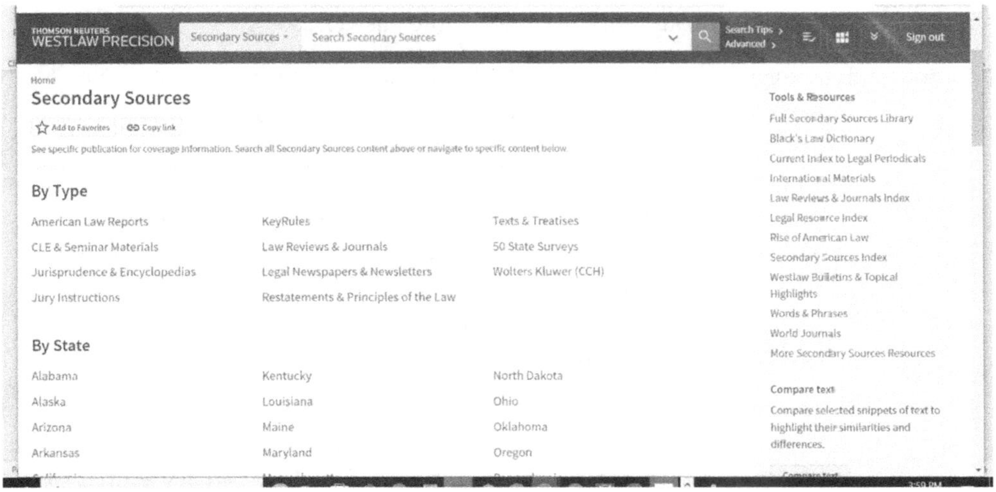

Figure 3.1 Searching Secondary Sources

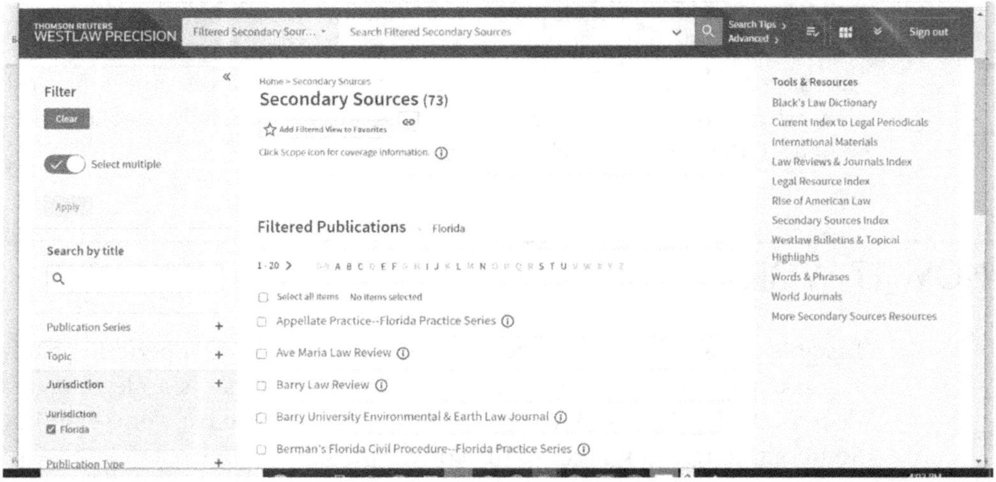

Figure 3.2 Filtering Secondary Sources

Examples

1. Your client wants to sue their employer because she believes it violated her rights when she was discriminated against after being sick with COVID-19 during the 2020 shutdown and having to miss work. There is no case on point that you know of, and you don't know where to look for information about such a suit. What steps should you take to find the law?
   a. Ask someone if they know anything about this issue.
   b. Google it or ask Siri.
   c. Review secondary sources and follow research steps.
   d. Look through old memos for the answer.

2. A former employee sues you for breach of contract in a complex business matter. There is a conflict in the case law governing this type of dispute. You cite the most recent edition of the Restatement of Contracts. Opposing counsel argues that the Restatement is not binding or even primary authority, therefore it does not apply. What is your response?
   a. Counsel is wrong and the court must follow it.
   b. The source could be helpful to the court.
   c. It does not matter one way or the other.
   d. There are some binding secondary sources.

3. The law regarding first-party insurance claims in your state has changed in recent years. A new client just received notice of a lawsuit against him filed by his own car insurance company. Which secondary source would be most helpful with getting up to date on the new law on that issue?

a. The Restatement of Torts
b. A treatise on national insurance law
c. Legal dictionaries
d. State-specific practice guides

4. Your legal research and writing professor hired you as a summer research assistant. She is working on an article about a new law in Texas regarding timesharing agreements in parenting plans. She asks you to find arguments of opponents and proponents of the new legislation. How will you do it?
   a. Search HeinOnline, legal research engines, and AI tools for secondary sources such as articles and other commentary on the law.
   b. Ask your friends and family what they have heard about it.
   c. Find news show recordings that discuss the issue.
   d. Make up arguments based on your own personal views.

5. In class, you are given a research question. It asks you to find the leading cases about housing discrimination in the United States. You are not familiar with the topic and don't know where to start. What would be the best source to get some basic knowledge?
   a. Find a primary source. Go through each case that comes up on the topic, one by one. The night is young.
   b. Locate a secondary source on the topic and see which cases are cited most frequently.
   c. Look for resources from the local housing authority.
   d. Ask an employee at the local housing authority.

Explanations

1. (a.) Incorrect. While asking another attorney could be helpful, you still must review the law for yourself. (b.) Incorrect. These methods are not the best practices for finding a legal answer. **(c.) Correct.** Choose a legal research engine. Find secondary sources. Review related articles that are found in the search. Click on cases, statutes, executive orders, or other primary authority within the readings. If available, create a folder to save all your findings. That may include an older case about an epidemic or an out-of-state case about someone with an illness or disability who was discriminated against at work. Because there is no on-point binding case, these persuasive sources could help. Based on the research, draft a legal memorandum or pleading that supports your case and is backed up by binding and persuasive sources found. (d.) Incorrect. Old memos will not be helpful for a new issue and fact pattern.

2. (a.) Incorrect. This is not the best answer. The court would expect an explanation as to how opposing counsel is wrong. **(b.) Correct.** While

it is true that the Restatement of Contracts is not primary authority and cannot be binding on any court, it clarifies the current view of the issue. It provides explanations and interpretations of the law in question. Even though no court has settled the conflict, this source can help the court understand and predict where the law might go. (c.) Incorrect. It actually does matter if a source is binding on the court. However, that does not mean the court cannot use it. This is not the best answer. (d.) Incorrect. This answer choice is not true. There are no secondary sources that are binding.

3. (a.) Incorrect. Restatements discuss basic doctrines of American law and are written by scholars. They may not be the best sources for such a specific issue. (b.) Incorrect. Treatises are more scholarly in nature and may not help with a practical, current issue. (c.) Incorrect. Legal dictionaries can assist you with the legal meaning of words but likely will not help with the current law. **(d.) Correct.** Practice guides are state-specific sources written by practitioners that guide lawyers. A current practice guide would be the most helpful secondary source in this situation.

4. **(a.) Correct.** This is the best answer. Secondary sources such as articles and amicus briefs written by practitioners and legal scholars commenting on new legislation would be the best way to find arguments on both sides. (b.) Incorrect. While friends and family may have heard of the new law, they may not have thought deeply enough for you to give proper arguments to your professor. (c.) Incorrect. While watching or listening to the news may be helpful, it reports on official arguments likely given by the same scholars and practitioners who author secondary sources. So, it is still best to get the arguments straight from the source. (d.) Incorrect. While your own opinions may align with one or both sides, you could be missing a crucial part of the arguments. This is not the best answer.

5. (a.) Incorrect. This is not the best answer. It would not be the most efficient use of time to view each case that may come up in a broad search. **(b.) Correct.** Reviewing secondary sources can help you learn the background on a topic and locate the leading cases on the issue. This is the best answer choice. (c.) Incorrect. The local housing authority may have some good information, but it is not the place to find case law. (d.) Incorrect. The employee at the housing authority may have some background knowledge but likely does not have the leading cases the professor asked for.

CHAPTER 4

Plan and Organize Your Research

WHERE DO I START?

Like almost anything else worth doing in life, you must have a plan. Research is no different. Once you have narrowed the legal question, it's best to make a research plan. Think about what sources you will use. Break down the legal question into specific tasks to be done. Identify the search terms to be used. Without a plan, you may find yourself getting bogged down with cases or other legal materials that are not helpful to your legal issue. Planning the direction of your research will make it organized, focused, and effective. At the very least, take notes on what has been researched so far and what research still needs to be done. That will keep you from going down a rabbit hole of cases that are not directly relevant to your issue. The research plan should include the factual scenario at hand, jurisdiction, possible search terms, dates of research, sources found, and notes on any clarifying questions you might have.

Start by answering the preliminary questions about your research topic. Likely, you've received a memo assignment or been given a fact pattern from a professor, supervisor, or client. They have asked you to answer a legal question. Like a reporter on the job, ask who, what, when, where, and why. Who are the key players? What is this case about? What are the details? What is the jurisdiction? What is the issue? When did the events take place? As a practicing attorney, you might also ask some additional questions. When are the filing deadlines? When are the hearing dates? Why is this case happening? Can or should it be settled? These questions will give you a focused approach to answering the legal question(s) and handling the case.

Imagine trying to answer a legal question without knowing these foundational elements. Without knowing which jurisdiction's laws to review, the question cannot confidently be answered. Without knowing when the events occurred, it is nearly impossible to determine if the cause of action is within the statute of limitations or if it happened while a certain law was in effect, for example. Who the parties are is also important. Certain rules may apply to corporations differently than individuals; private companies and governmental agencies may be treated differently as well. The relationship between parties and the age of a party could also impact a case. For example, in a criminal case, a battery on an elderly person or pregnant person may carry a harsher punishment. An assault between family members may be a different charge.

In practice, filing deadlines will be important because in some areas of law, certain motions or charging documents may need to be filed by a particular statutory deadline. Knowing a client's motive for wanting to file a lawsuit could also help in settlement or mediation negotiations and save some research time. For example, if a client just wants someone to stop doing something or to take something seriously but not necessarily go to court, a letter from a lawyer may suffice. If a lawsuit is filed and settlement is possible or preferred, having leading cases will help determine if there is leverage for settlement based on the client's facts and case precedent. So, asking the right questions determines the course of action and makes for efficient and effective research.

Think about what you already know from the facts and preliminary research. Determine if there are leading cases or statutes that govern the particular area of law. A leading case is one that sets legal precedent. *Miranda v. Arizona* (1966) is a famous leading case. Based on the U.S. Supreme Court's decision, anyone in police custody must be read the *Miranda* rights that we've all heard on famous police procedurals like *Law & Order*.

By using the search functions that we discussed in Chapters 2 and 3, you can determine what the leading cases are for your specific research topic because these cases will be cited often in secondary sources and other case law. When conducting such searches, be sure to consider if there are any synonyms to your search terms that may help get more results. Think about the case on both sides. What claims would or could you bring? What are the defenses? What relief is being sought?

ORGANIZING ONLINE

After gathering answers to all the previous questions, get organized. Traditionally, attorneys would create a physical folder with printed copies of case law, notes, and other legal material. That practice is still done by some, but there are also several popular ways to organize online.

4. Plan and Organize Your Research

As you research, keep notes. Write down the steps already taken and the next steps. Make notes on cases you've reviewed and search terms. Comment on sources you've found and how they might be useful. Notes can be taken on paper or using notetaking software such as OneNote or similar apps. Using Westlaw folders online is another method. There is no wrong way to do it, but some methods are more efficient than others. Notetaking will ensure that you do not keep searching the same terms or taking repetitive steps. It will let you pick up where you left off when returning to research after a break.

When creating folders on Westlaw, subfolders can also be created. For example, if you are researching for a negligence issue, the main folder may be titled "Negligence" but subfolders within that folder may be titled "Causation" or "Duty." Each folder would contain cases and other material pertaining to that issue or subissue. Most online legal research engines have a similar system. But when in court or for an oral argument, it is not always feasible to take all your notes or sort through all the folders when looking for an answer to a question. In this case, it is best to make a condensed version of your research. It can be a legal pad or printout with bullet points of your arguments or case briefs with highlights so you can quickly find information in case it escapes your memory during live arguments.

HOW IT WORKS

Once a case of interest is found on Westlaw, click on the folder icon that is currently located at the top right corner of the page (Figure 4.1). From there,

Figure 4.1 Select Folder

name the folder and the case will be added to that folder (Figure 4.2). Click on the plus signs below the main folder to create subfolders (Figure 4.3). Important text or language in the cases can also be highlighted or notated within the case (Figure 4.4).

You can also save notes to yourself that pertain to the text of the case. See Figures 4.5 and 4.6.

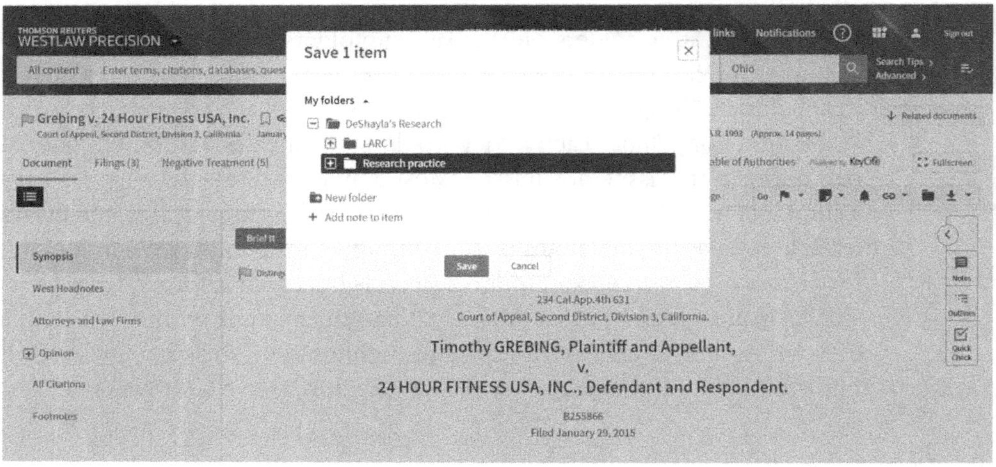

Figure 4.2 Name Folder

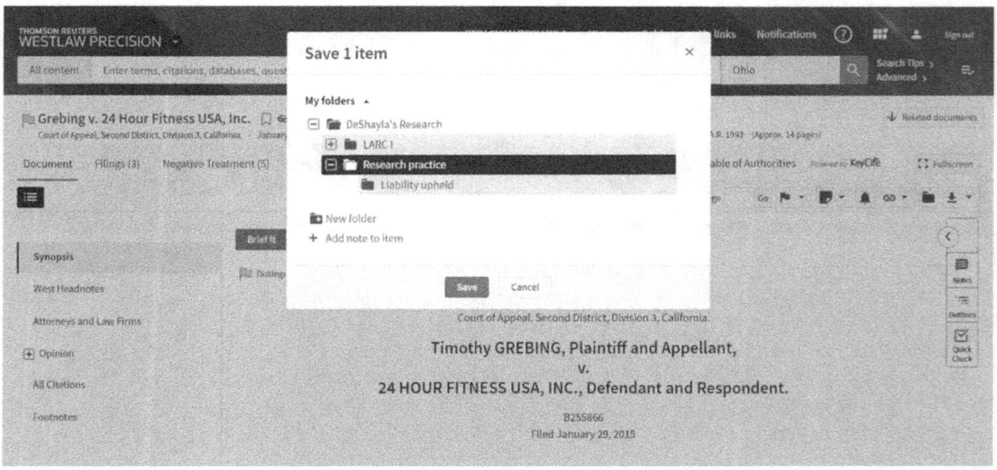

Figure 4.3 Create Subfolders

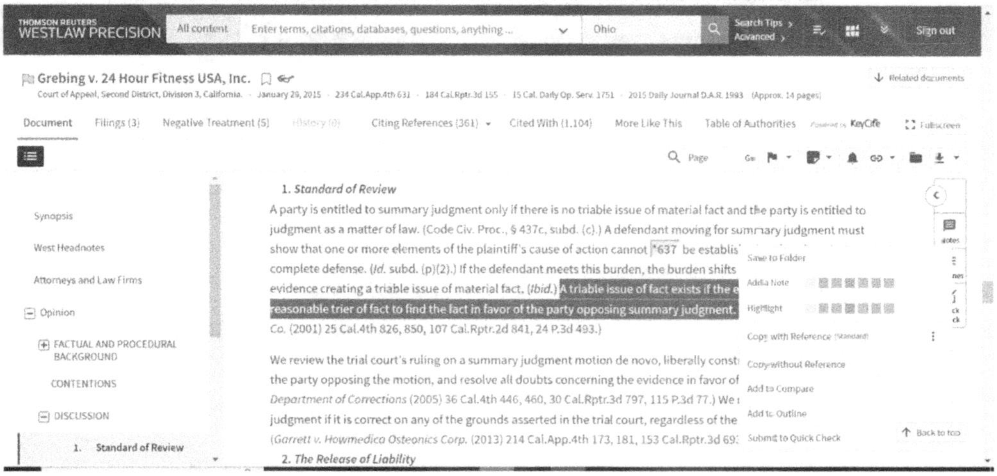

Figure 4.4 Highlight Text

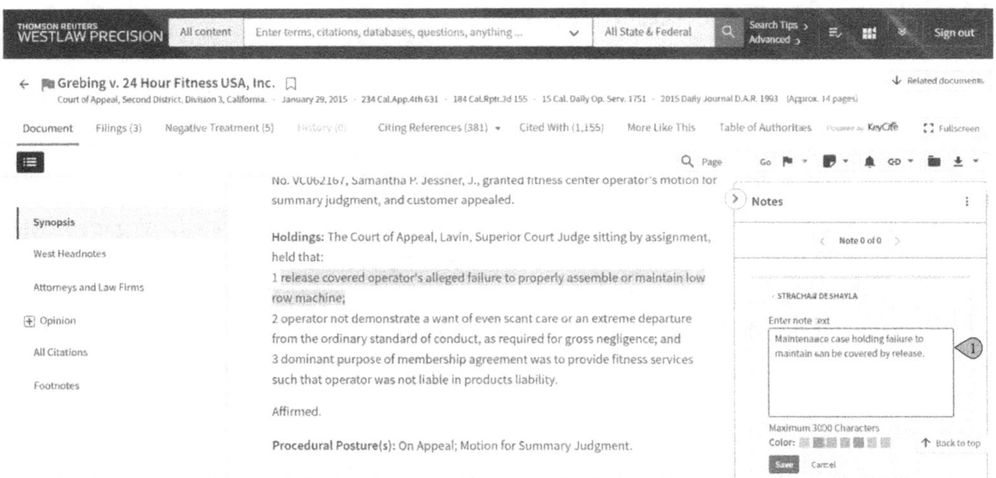

(1) Note

Figure 4.5 Enter Note

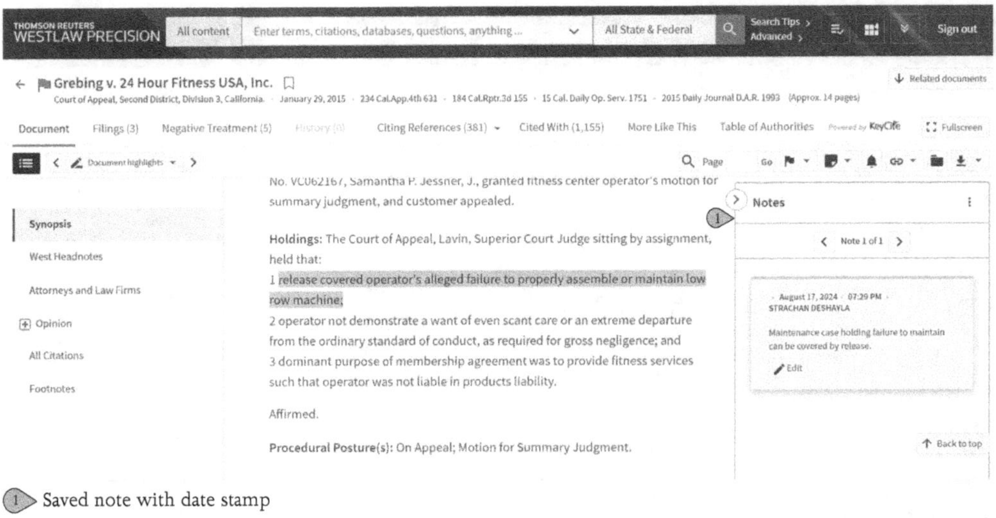

Figure 4.6 Remember to Save Notes

MAKING A RESEARCH PLAN

The best way to organize your research plan is to get it down on paper (whether virtual or not). A written plan will help you be more efficient in your research and can save valuable time. It will help you see where you need to go and what you already have. In your plan, include the jurisdiction, the case facts, the issues, what you already know about the law, any gaps in the law, and sources used. Keep track of search terms and results. For an example, see the sample Research Plan and sample Research Notes below. Any notes can be added to the end or beginning of the research plan. For some, an Excel spreadsheet or online notepad works best for their process. Others may still choose to use good ol' pen and paper to keep up with their research. Notes may look similar to a research plan but less organized. You may choose to just use one or the other or combine them by including notes in the plan.

Case charts and features charts are a great way to organize the wealth of cases found from hours of researching. Case charts organize cases by their facts, arguments, holding, reasoning, disposition, and source of law. Features charts organize cases by breaking down the facts and features of each case. You can see a sample Case Chart and Case Features Chart below. Once done, that will help determine what the overall or synthesized rule of law is and which cases should be used for certain issues. Rule synthesis is the process of combining rules from multiple cases to identify the law and answer a legal question. It focuses on generalizations of case facts and the court's reasoning. These charts will also be helpful when needing to compare and distinguish cases in legal memos and oral arguments.

Research Plan

Deadline: March 30, 20xx
Client name: Jane Doe

Facts:

Who? [list parties involved]
What? [what events happened that gave rise to this action? State background and legally significant facts]
Where? [name the jurisdiction]
When? [dates of the event and other important dates]
Issues presented? [state the legal issues that arise from these facts or the legal question given to answer]
What do I already know about these issues? What do I need to know?

Research:

- Search terms - [identify words to search and synonyms, queries, and questions]
- Review secondary sources - [law journals, annotated statutes, etc.]
- Review primary sources - [cases, statutes, and regulations]

Track and Update:

- Keep track of the dates of your research, search terms, and sources found.
- Take notes and save sources in online folders.
- Make sure all sources are good law.

Figure 4.7 Research Plan

Research Notes

Facts: Client said she slipped and fell on an unknown liquid in the store last month. She hurt her hip.

Issue: Whether store owner was negligent
Parties and witnesses: client, her sister, her child, and another customer, store owner
Applicable law: Georgia common law

Negligence elements - duty, breach of duty, actual cause, proximate cause, harm

Search -> slip/trip and fall in Georgia, duty to store invitees, negligence of store owner

Additional questions: Was it raining? Did anyone else slip? Any caution signs up?

Need: case law, statutes?

Figure 4.8 Research Notes

Case Chart: Intentional Infliction of Emotional Distress

Case Citation	Legally Significant Facts Re: IIED	Parties' Legal Arguments Re: IIED (Appellant/ Respondent)	Court's Disposition Re: IIED (affirmed, reversed, etc.)	Court's Holding Re: IIED	Court's Reasoning Re: IIED	Source of Law Judge Applied (Statutes, Cases, Mixture)	Method of Reasoning (statutory language, precedent, policy, combination)

Figure 4.9 Case Chart

Features Chart: Intentional Infliction of Emotional Distress

Factual Categories	**Marks (1999)**	**Browley (2005)**	**Smith (2001)**	**Diaz-Perez (1998)**	**Venetia (1995)**	**Generalization**
What physical signs of emotional distress did the P exhibit?						Example: One factor a court relies on in determining IIED is the physical manifestations of distress
Where did the conduct happen?						
Who observed the conduct?						
What was the conduct that caused the IIED?						When conduct is considered extreme and outrageous, courts tend to find IIED
Who observed physical signs of distress?						
To what extent did the court rely on signs of emotional distress?						
[additional category of facts that would be worth tracking?]						

Figure 4.10 Case Features Chart

Examples

1. The research problem you have been assigned has three issues. The client was injured skiing but he signed a liability release. To enforce the release, the ski resort must show that the release was clear, the injury was within the scope of the release, and the release did not violate public policy. There is an overwhelming number of cases that apply to each issue. Some of the cases could be used for multiple issues. What should you do to keep it all straight?
   a. Just use the search history to find each case you read.
   b. Print them all so you can go through them later.
   c. Highlight important language in each case, make notes on the cases with online sticky notes, and organize the cases in folders, making a folder for each issue.
   d. Make physical binders for each issue.

2. Oral arguments are coming up. You have written your brief but need an abbreviated version to take to "court." What should you bring?
   a. Your computer because it has all your research and your brief to refer to, but nothing else
   b. A simple folder, notepad, or tablet with a page or two of brief bulleted notes, and your computer as backup
   c. Several hundred pages of case law that have been bound for ease of review
   d. Nothing. Arguments should be done from memory alone.

3. In a closed-universe memo, the professor has assigned seven cases for your review. You must only use these cases in this single-issue memo. They are all pertaining to intentional infliction of emotional distress. Some cases are better for your fictional case than others. What's the best way to organize?
   a. Make a case chart that has the facts, issues, holding, and reasoning. That way you can highlight the cases that best illustrate the issue in your case.
   b. Make a flowchart to show which cases work best.
   c. Make a line graph of the cases.
   d. Just have each case saved in Westlaw and you can pull it up when needed.

4. When starting to work on a new case, your supervisor gives you the facts of the case and asks you to do some research and report your results in a memo. You spend the rest of the day researching and will pick up where

you left off tomorrow. What is the best way to remember the work done today and what still needs to be done?
a. Westlaw folders
b. The handwritten notes taken while speaking to the supervisor
c. The history on the research engine
d. Making a research plan

EXPLANATIONS

Explanations

1. (a.) Incorrect. Using the search history function is certainly helpful to find cases you have reviewed but it is not the best way to organize research. It does not allow a way to sort cases effectively. (b.) Incorrect. Printing the cases is one way to do it but without an organization system, that could still be overwhelming and heavy! It could be hundreds of pages. **(c.) Correct.** Making notes and highlights within the document and placing cases in a specified folder is the best answer here. It allows an efficient way to find cases you plan to rely on for each issue. You could also make subfolders for mini-issues within the main issue. Here, you could make a folder for clarity, a folder for scope, and a folder for public policy. Put cases that have decisions on each issue in its specific folder. Some cases may end up in all folders if a case has a holding on each issue. (d.) Incorrect. Like the (b.) answer choice, printing cases and making binders is a way to go but may be more cumbersome than it's worth.

2. (a.) Incorrect. This could work but is not the best answer. Bringing a computer is good for backup in case you need to do quick research on a break in court but not to read verbatim from your research engines. **(b.) Correct.** When going to oral arguments or court, it is best to keep your materials as simple as possible. That way you are not tempted to read or constantly rummage and scroll through documents. Having a short page or two of notes on paper or on a tablet is the most manageable way to keep track of your arguments. You may also have your laptop computer just in case you are asked a question not in your notes or memory, or you are tasked with looking something up on the spot. (c.) Incorrect. This is not the best answer for reasons discussed above. Going through pages of case law and notes can be frustrating to the court and make you appear unorganized or unprepared. It could also make it tempting to read these documents instead of simply stating the law and facts as you know them. (d.) Incorrect. This is also not the best approach. Having nothing with you in court or at oral argument can leave you always saying, "I'll get back to you on that, your honor," because you've been asked something you cannot recall, or the name of a case escapes you.

3. **(a.) Correct.** Case charts and features charts are a quick and easy way to organize your research. They help you visualize and conceptualize each case. That will help you when synthesizing the law and deciding how to use each case. (b.) Incorrect. Flowcharts are not the best way to organize legal research. They are best when diagramming a process but may not work as well with legal research. (c.) Incorrect. Line graphs are also not the best way to organize legal research. These work best with math or data when showing how something changes over time. (d.) Incorrect. Saving the cases in a research engine is helpful and necessary but is not the most efficient way to organize. When writing the memo you will need to constantly refer to the cases. So, having to click around Westlaw may take longer than glancing at your chart.

4. (a.) Incorrect. Westlaw or Lexis folders are helpful if cases are saved there but they will not tell you the exact legal questions you were trying to answer with those cases. (b.) Incorrect. Handwritten notes may also be helpful if they are thorough and organized. But chances are they are not. Conversations with supervising attorneys are often brief and there may not have been ample time to take enough notes. (c.) Incorrect. The search history can be helpful but is not the best way to organize your research. **(d.) Correct.** This is the best answer. Creating a research plan as you begin your research will keep you clear and organized. It is a good way to document the facts, legal question, jurisdiction, notes, and research done thus far.

CHAPTER 5

Research Engines and New Technology

RESEARCH ENGINES

Most lawyers use online legal research engines to conduct research. One can search for cases, statutes, and other legal materials on these user-friendly search engines that contain a large database of up-to-date primary and secondary sources, as mentioned in Chapters 2 and 3. The main commercial research providers are Westlaw and Lexis. These are very helpful but come at a large cost. For this reason, many law firms and solo practitioners turn to free or less expensive legal research engines to cut costs. But with low cost comes limitations. Fee-based research engines offer a wider range of legal materials and more features to aid research endeavors. A lawyer may work for a big law firm or government agency that pays for Westlaw or Lexis, but a solo practitioner just starting out may not be able to afford the extra overhead. Therefore, someone in such a position must rely on free or low-cost databases. Fastcase (which you have access to with state bar membership), FindLaw, and Google Scholar are primary alternatives to the expensive well-known databases.

At this stage in your legal career, it might not be possible to know if your first legal position will be with a big law firm, a smaller firm, or even as a solo practitioner. That's why it is important to learn how to find the information you need without relying on the above-mentioned major research engines. Because some law firms may not have access to Westlaw or Lexis or any new technology, it is a good idea to become comfortable researching on alternative search engines so you are fully prepared. In any case, researching on any platform comes down to search techniques. The search terms that are used and how they are connected play a large part in the results returned. Searching with natural language may do the trick. Natural language searches contain the same words you would use in an everyday conversation—typing a simple question just as you would do on any other non-legal search engine. For example, "What are the laws in Arizona on squatters?" is a natural language search question that may return helpful results. Using natural language rather than specific legal language allows the computer to interpret what is stated and return results. We discuss search terms and techniques in more detail in Chapter 9.

NEW TECHNOLOGY

A responsible lawyer has a duty to stay up to date on research methods, as well as to work in the most efficient ways possible to lighten the financial burden on clients. As new technology is developing rapidly, this idea might seem daunting. Relax and remember that your research skills are not dependent on specific pieces of technology. As long as you remember to be careful and to critically analyze whatever your research brings up, you can take on whatever new form of research technology comes your way.

One such development in recent years is the use of artificial intelligence, and specifically generative AI. As many lawyers and law firms turn to the use of generative AI, it's a good idea to know what you're dealing with: how it can help your research, and what to look out for.

What Is Generative AI?

In November 2022, generative artificial intelligence was introduced to the legal community when OpenAI, an AI research company, released ChatGPT as a free "research preview."

Generative AI is a large language model that processes vast amounts of information on the internet and uses it to create text, images, and data. These AI tools, like ChatGPT, can help you navigate through large amounts of information and help serve as a foundation to research if used correctly and ethically. It can introduce you to cases, statutes, and other sources of information. However, proceed with caution. Just as online legal research engines continue to update, AI engines do as well. So, the researcher must make sure they are using the latest version of the AI platform to ensure that their research is as up to date as possible. Even more important, the researcher has a responsibility to check the accuracy of the output and edit it as needed.

The most significant issue with using AI is that these large language models can sometimes hallucinate, making up things as they try to predict the next word. They synthesize content and patterns to sound plausible, but the output is not always reality. For example, in *Mata v. Avianca* (2023), a man sued an airline for damage sustained to his knee during a flight. In court, lawyers representing the man submitted a brief citing numerous legal precedents to support their case. But there was one problem: none of the cases existed! The attorney had used ChatGPT to write the brief and ChatGPT made up all of the cases. This case gained public attention due to the negligence of the lawyer.

So, a human must always carefully check and edit AI-generated research and content. But in spite of any potential negative views of AI, the truth is that the technology is here, is being used by people around you, and if used, it must be used ethically.

Large language models read everything that is free and available on the internet. They are trained by professionals and use their own browsing and protocols. Think of AI as an assistant or a tool to use. It is not a lawyer. It has knowledge but not opinions or a human touch. It often gives incomplete information or provides weak sources, if any. It is up to the researcher to make judgments and to put the AI output into context. At the time of this writing, non-legal AI engines, such as ChatGPT, do not always provide citations or sources unless asked to do so. That is why it is even more important to verify its output before using it in any legal work. Legal AI, such as Lexis+ AI, does provide sources and cases but often does not provide enough cases or binding case law. That is why it is important to understand legal research before using tools like AI, because when you know what types of sources should be produced, you can tell when improper sources are given. It is also important to note that non-legal AI products have fewer guardrails than AI products made for lawyers. Products such as ChatGPT search vast amounts of information on the internet. In contrast, legal AI products, such as Westlaw and Lexis+, have more protection and are less likely to grab extraneous information off the internet by mistake due to having their own longstanding research databases.

Using Artificial Intelligence as a Research Aid

Many new AI engines are being created and updated as you read. Ghostwriter Legal AI, LegalGPT, and CoCounsel (now West's) are examples of specialized legal AI. These are among the more than 30 AI chatbots that are currently available. Law firms have also begun to incorporate AI tools into their own case management systems in order to protect client proprietary information. There are certain aspects of using AI that lawyers in particular must keep in mind. In practice, lawyers must take care not to put confidential client information or case strategy into AI chatbots, in case these chatbots reuse the data they receive. When typing in queries, never use client names. The conversation with the chatbot should be general and not disclose confidential information. Copyright protection could also be a concern when using ChatGPT responses or inputting your own work into the chatbot. The response may be using a creator's original work and should not be replicated verbatim in your writings. Generally, attorneys must supervise the work of AI just as they supervise the work of anyone in their employ.

Queries must be accurate to receive the best responses. The best responses come from the best queries. Chatting with any AI chatbot is a conversation. It can be asked to generate, revise, and use specific tones or points of view. Researchers can give feedback to describe accuracy and adherence to the prompt. It is helpful for brainstorming and summarizing text. AI tools can help organize writing and synthesize ideas and case law. But the first step to a good AI response is a well-crafted prompt. We will discuss what makes a good prompt below.

This focus on the prompt is particularly important for public AI engines which draw on huge quantities of data. You can use that type of generative AI for legal research but stay aware that such engines were not created specifically for legal research. For example, the latest version of ChatGPT can produce good responses, but they do not automatically come with citations. So, again, much more fact checking is involved. Gemini is Google's AI software tool, akin to ChatGPT. Formerly known as Bard, it promises to help with writing, planning, learning, and more. When tested, it seems to do the same job as other non-legal AI chatbots. Enter a prompt and it fetches information from other sources, like Google's services. A researcher must have a personal Google account to access Gemini. Another disadvantage to note about these public AI engines is that the language models can generate biased responses. Biases are usually caused by lack of data and gaps in training. There may be limitations on their answers about certain countries, cultures, or ethnicities—even more reason to always check the answers you receive.

LegalGPT launched in 2024. It specializes in legal matters and promises to assist legal professionals with case research, legal documentation, and predicting case outcomes based on historical data. It is built on the foundation of ChatGPT 3.5 and is free of charge. It does not appear to be any more accurate than its GPT counterpart, but it provides a useful foundation of research to the lawyer. It only focuses on legal issues, and it displays the sites it searched to retrieve its output. That will allow the researcher to review additional sources for a more complete search.

But there have also been AI systems created specifically for lawyers, using existing legal research sites. In 2023, Lexis+ AI was introduced to legal skills faculty. Westlaw Precision with generative AI soon followed, introducing its product to faculty in early 2024. These updates in the popular legal research engines promised AI-assisted research to practitioners and law students. That means when conducting online legal research the search engines will analyze the content of the site to generate answers, much like they already do and have done for decades, but now responses are more specific to the question asked. Based on the query, a new and specific response will populate in real time instead of a prewritten response.

But even with these lawyer-specific AI tools, it is still important to think about the risks involved when choosing AI engines. Even with legal AI, case holdings have been misstated and sources have been lacking. In a recent Stanford study, it was found that Lexis+ AI hallucinates 17 percent of the time and Westlaw's AI-powered research hallucinates 33 percent of the time. The study also found that Lexis+ AI provided accurate answers 65 percent of the time, while Westlaw provided accurate answers 42 percent of the time. That does not mean that the research companies are inaccurate the rest of the time, because there are some instances where answers were unresponsive or lacked grounding. But it is even more proof that AI should be used sparingly and with much caution, even when it is designed for a specific purpose.

With Westlaw and Lexis+, citations are included, and you can even ask them to summarize a case for you—though you should always check your answers, as seen above. CoCounsel goes one step further and asserts that it protects confidentiality. At the minimum, AI can act as a secondary source when the researcher has a case of first impression or no knowledge of the subject area. It can possibly save a layer of research. Because legal AI will review secondary and primary sources, it can at least give you the correct terminology and direction to continue researching.

But as we have seen, there are numerous caveats to using AI in your research. For one, most AI companies update their information quarterly or annually, so the information given is likely not up to date. Pro Se litigants utilizing AI must also be aware of inaccuracies that may appear in responses. Using AI might seem easier and faster but the answers must be checked against current state statutes and local ordinances. So, it's best to go straight to the sources in the first place if you are able to. Review recent cases cited on free legal research engines to make certain the cases are real and apply to your legal situation. The bottom line is that AI can make lawyers more efficient and increase access to justice for the layperson. It saves time by gathering information from several sources and synthesizing data. It summarizes and organizes, and it can give you a valuable overview of areas of law that you are unfamiliar with. But because there is such a need to verify its output, and ethical considerations, it may not always save as much time as originally thought. These large language models should only be thought of and utilized as a foundation to research, just as a secondary source but with a higher need for editing and fact checking. It is only a starting point. Remember, AI is not a substitute for the research process. It is a great new technology but is not infallible. You will still need to do much more research to get a full understanding of the nuances and verify the accuracy of the summaries produced.

Things that must be checked in an AI response:

- Citations—Citations must be in proper format (i.e., Bluebook form).
- Cases—Cases must be real and not hallucinated.
- Currentness—Cases must be good law.
- Hierarchy—Cases must be useable (i.e., published and preferably binding).

Costs

Something to consider when choosing research engines and AI tools is the cost-benefit analysis. Fee-based AI bots range from free versions with limited functionality to paid versions that can do much more. The paid version of ChatGPT currently costs $20 per month. Ghostwriter AI Legal currently costs a one-time fee of $250. Lexis+ AI currently starts at $861 per month in addition to the minimum $140 monthly subscription. Alexi, another legal AI platform, starts at $99 per user per month. Westlaw Precision AI costs depend on the firm size and jurisdiction. A one-year plan for a solo practitioner in Florida will set you back $306 per month. These fees are subject to change periodically.

Lexis+ AI

The AI-assisted research on Lexis+ has a similar model to most other AI chatbots (Figure 5.1). The researcher will first filter to the correct jurisdiction. Then, the platform has options to ask a legal question or generate a draft. It will even give examples of legal questions to ask. Some benefits of Lexis+ AI are that it can summarize cases, summarize text, draft documents, answer legal questions, and provide links to its sources.

It promises to accelerate research tasks. You can ask a legal question regarding case law, statutory codes, practical guidance, or treatises. It will even provide prompting tips to the researcher so it can give the best response (Figure 5.2). It reminds researchers to review for accuracy.

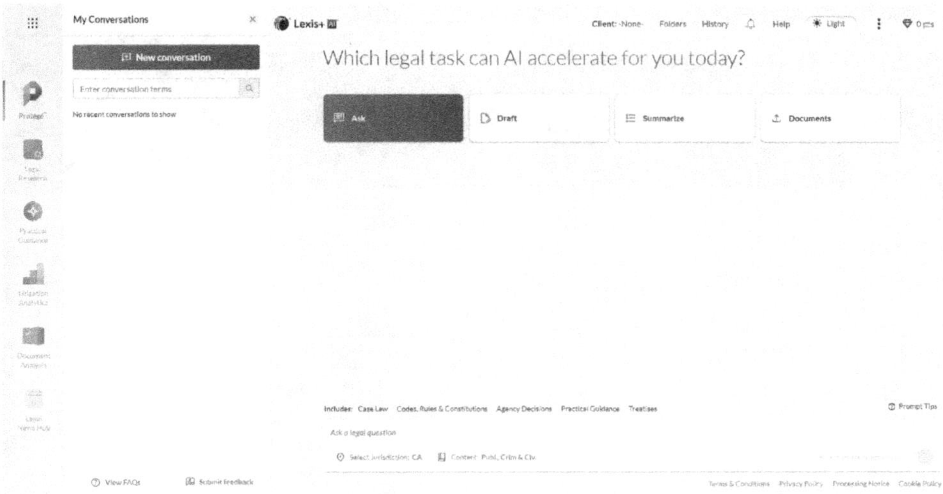

Figure 5.1 Lexis+ AI

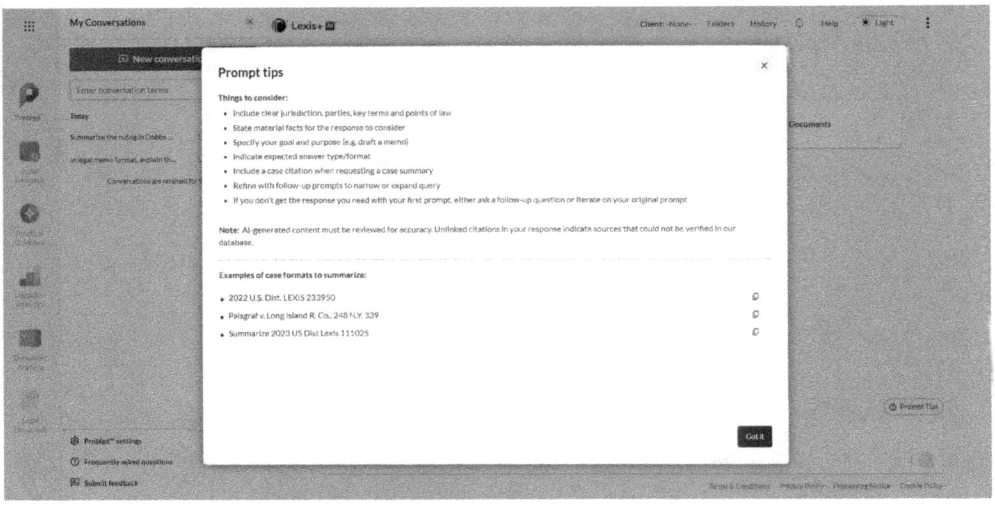

Figure 5.2 Lexis+ AI Prompting Tips

Westlaw Precision with AI-assisted Research

Similar to Lexis+ AI, Westlaw provides AI-assisted research through its product Westlaw Precision with CoCounsel (Figure 5.3). Combining generative AI with its already vast database, the company promises to deliver an intuitive experience and answer legal questions even faster. Students

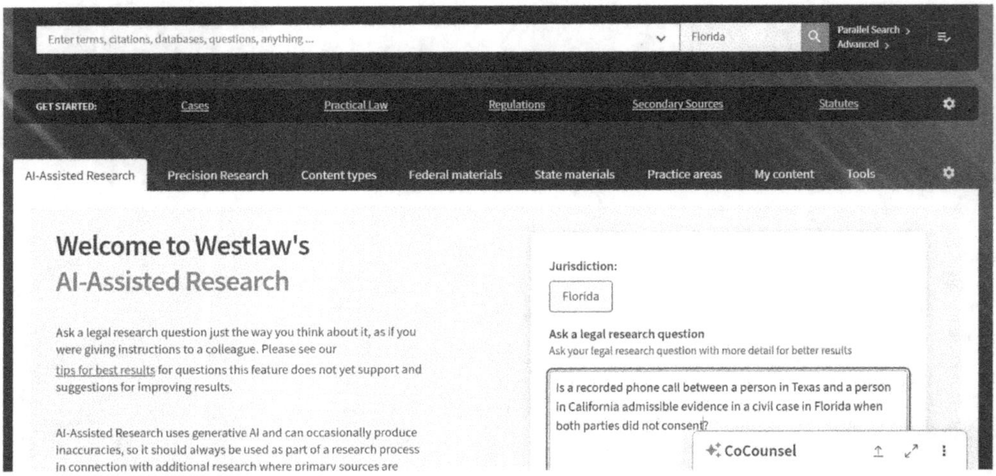

Figure 5.3 Westlaw AI-Assisted Research

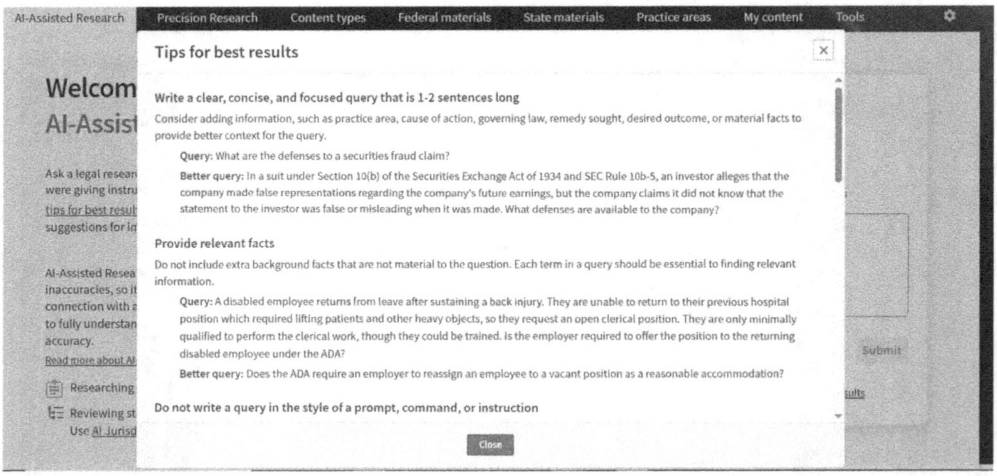

Figure 5.4 Tips for Best Results

and practitioners can simply ask a question in everyday plain language and receive a relevant answer generated only from Westlaw content. It also provides tips on writing the best queries to produce the most accurate output (Figure 5.4). A disclaimer about possible inaccuracies is also included as a reminder for researchers to review cases for themselves.

Westlaw's AI addition comes with many other key features that will help with finding and organizing research (Figure 5.5). That includes a parallel search feature, which finds relevant cases using similar words from your original search. The Graphical View of History feature lets researchers see

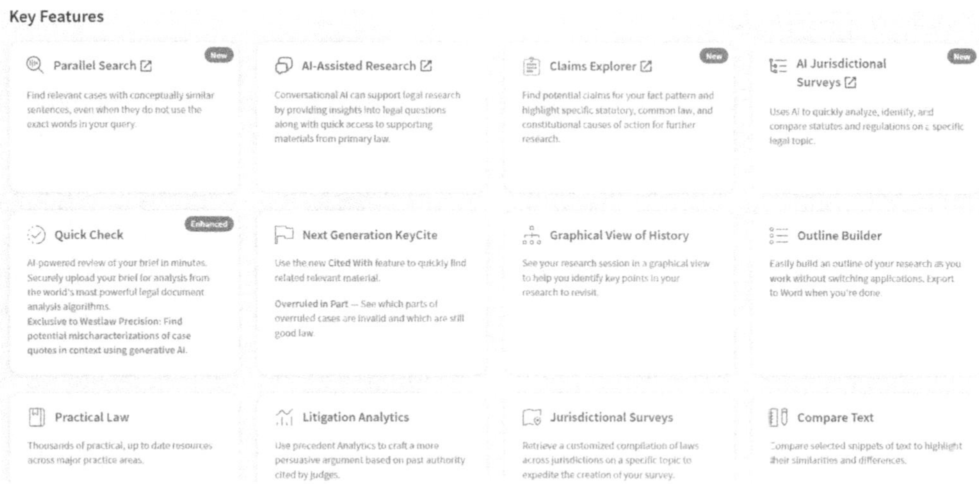

Figure 5.5 Key Features

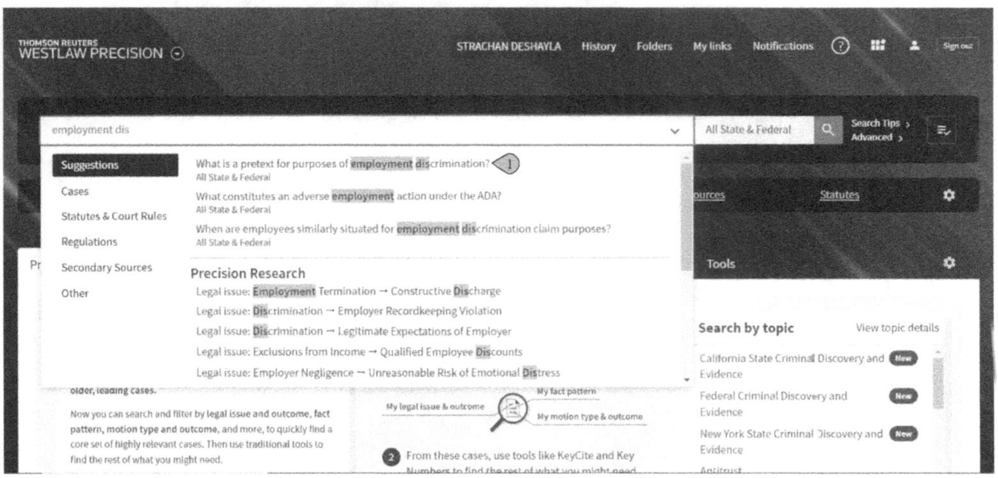

(1) Predictive questions

Figure 5.6 Predictive Questions

their research from a graphical point of view that highlights key points that may need revisiting. The outline builder feature creates an outline of your research that can then be exported to a Word document.

In addition to the new AI features, keep in mind that Westlaw also can help you with predictive questions. Simply start to enter a term or question into the global search bar and select the most relevant query served up by the predictive question tool (Figure 5.6).

Prompt Engineering

To get the best, most helpful responses from AI, you need to come up with a good question. The more specific the query, the better the answer. Be as specific as you can in your query without giving away confidential client information. Remember that it is more like a conversation. The query should be at least one or two sentences long. Tell the chatbot the jurisdiction, key terms, and the cause of action. Consider also adding the remedy sought and material facts to give more context. Focus on a single issue or ask separate questions. Do not combine multiple questions into one sentence. For example, asking it, "What is the law on abortion in Montana when the mother is a minor?" is better than asking, "What is the law on abortion?"

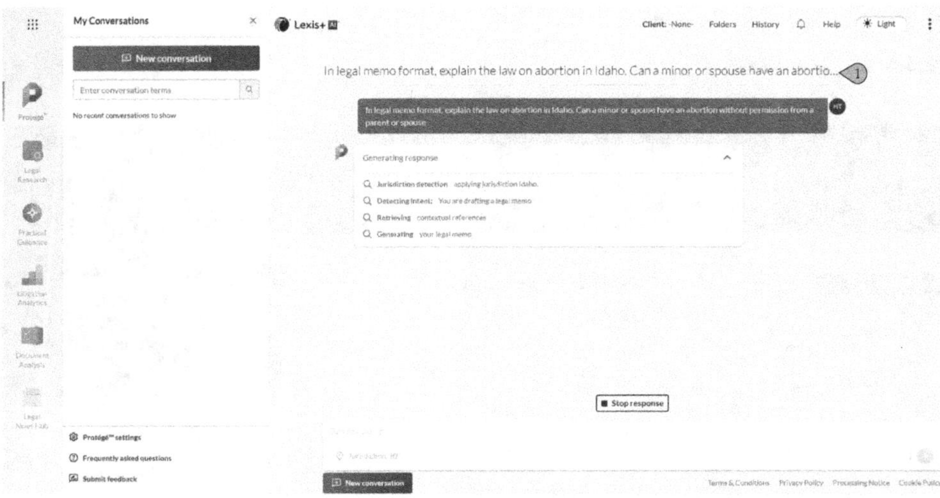

1 Prompt

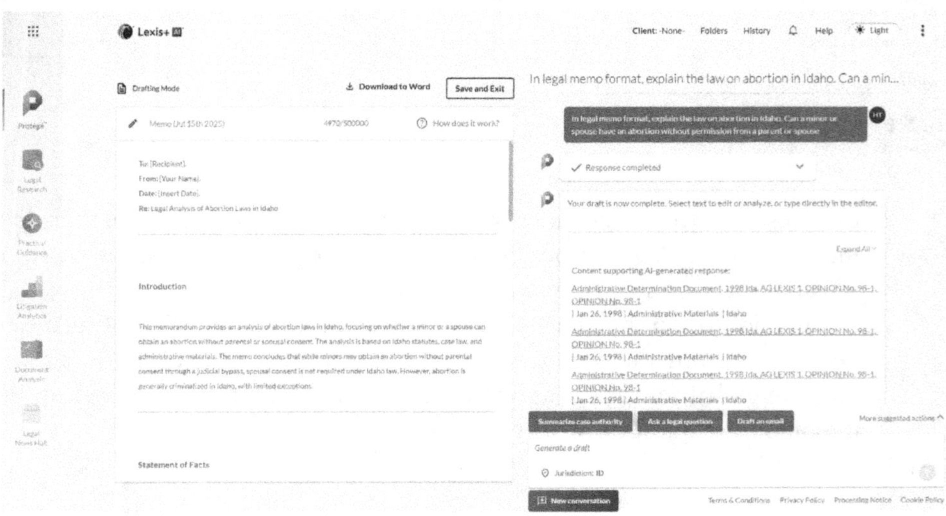

Figure 5.7 Prompts for AI Using Lexis

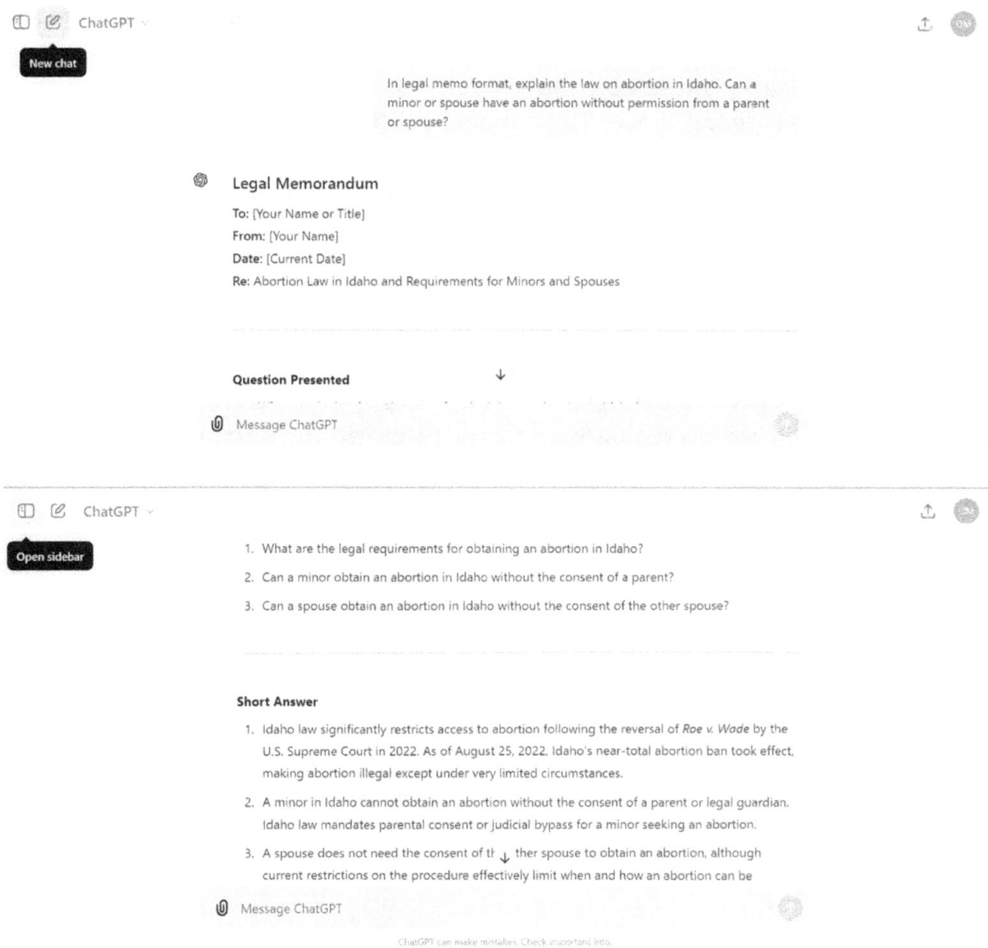

Figure 5.8 Prompts for AI Using ChatGPT

HOW IT WORKS

To begin using AI, simply sign up for an AI platform such as ChatGPT. Most will have free membership but offer a more sophisticated paid version as well. Sign up online or on its mobile application. Type a question or prompt into the chatbox. The system will then generate a response based on its understanding of the input language. The response comes from information found on online sources up to a certain year. Once a response is generated, the user can then like or dislike it, copy the response, or ask the program to regenerate it. If the user asks the chatbot to regenerate a response, the user can then tell the chatbot if the second response was better, worse, or the same.

For example, after reviewing a case given to you in an open-universe memo assignment, you want to see if there are more cases like it. The case is very long. In an AI chatbox, you can ask it to summarize the case and give you more cases like it. Then, review the summary and cases. Check the case names and citations in a traditional legal research engine. Continue researching from there. The response can be rated based on its adherence to the prompt and accuracy. If the user is not happy with the answer, it can rate the response with thumbs down or ask it to regenerate the response. That information will help in training the AI model.

As another example, let's assume that as an attorney you are given a unique fact scenario in a family law matter. The issue is not one that has been handled in your jurisdiction before. Typing the general facts in AI and asking for the answer to the legal question could give you a starting point and send you in the right direction to begin your research.

The various responses to this fact scenario are examined below:

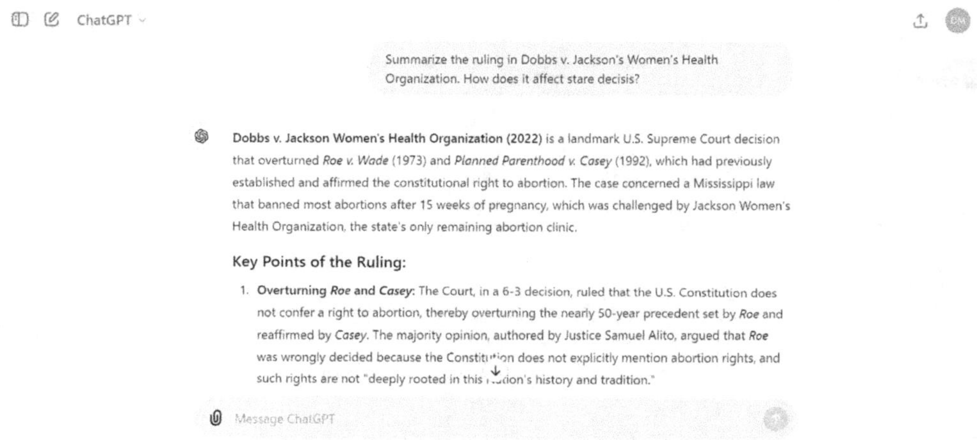

Figure 5.9 ChatGPT Case Summary

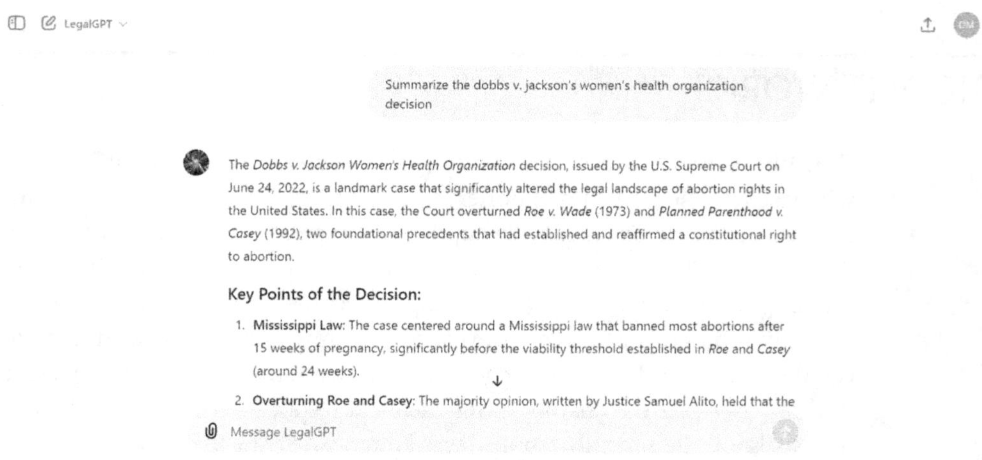

Figure 5.10 LegalGPT Case Summary

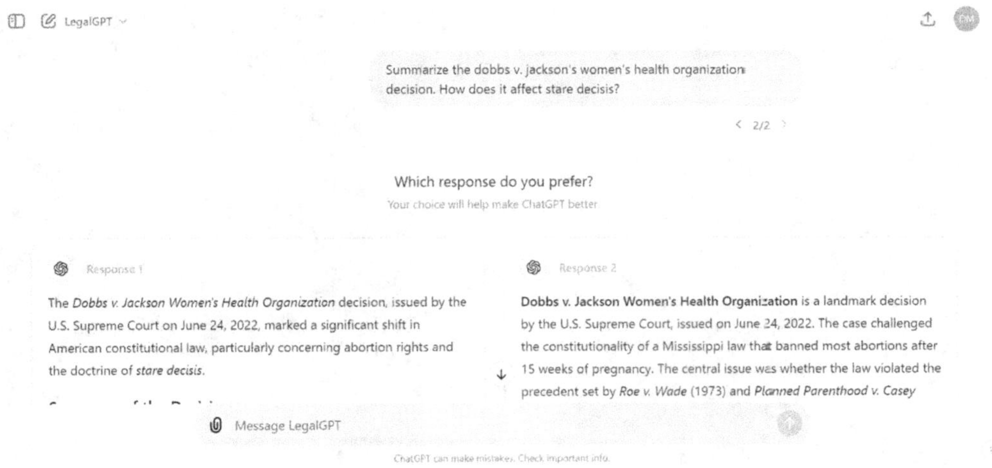

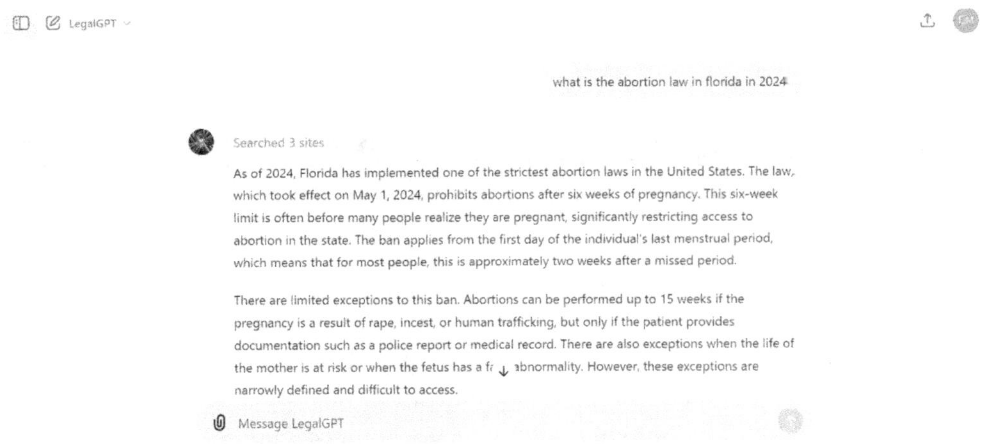

Figure 5.10 Continued

As you see, the response is not much different than the non-legal GPT case summary. However, it does offer choices based on two responses to the same prompt.

The responses between Lexis and Gemini are also similar. However, Lexis provides links to the case law being discussed. While, in Westlaw's Co-Counsel AI-assisted research, the AI assistant states that the question is outside of its scope. Tips for better queries are provided.

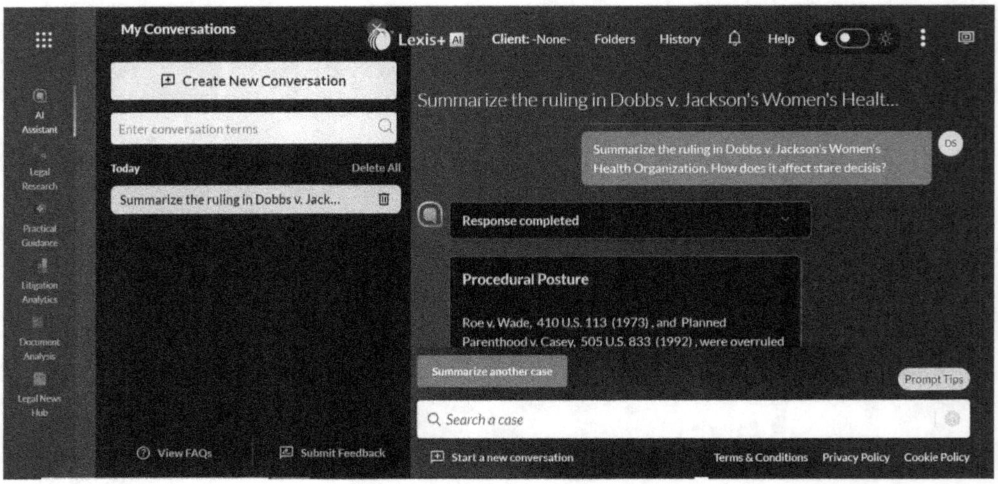

Figure 5.11 Lexis+ AI Case Summary

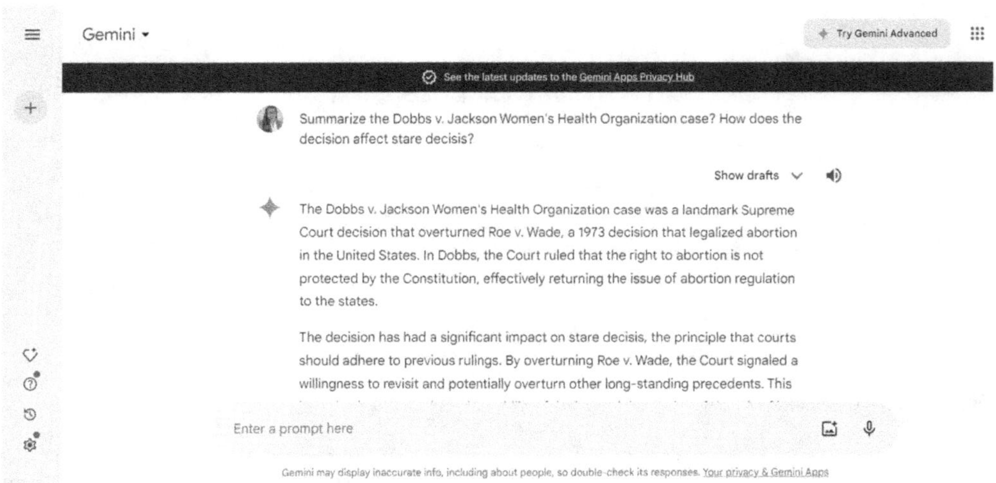

Figure 5.12 Gemini Case Summary

Examples

1. Your supervising attorney asks about the DUI and DWI (driving under the influence/driving while intoxicated) laws in Texas. He has not given you any law to review. He requests a memo explaining the law and assessing the strength of a client's case. Which of the following are the correct next steps?
   a. Ask ChatGPT to find the answer for you and send your supervisor the response.

   b. Research the answer in secondary sources, find corresponding case law and statutes, review, and write the memo.
   c. Look up Texas statutes online and find what the DUI/DWI statutes say and send the link to your supervisor.
   d. Find an article that references the Texas laws on Google Scholar.

2. A client emails you for an update on his personal injury case. He lets you know about the new back pain he is having and wants to know what the next steps are. What query would be best to put in an AI chatbot?
   a. "Client personal injury update letter"
   b. "Personal injury case update with back pain"
   c. "Florida car accident case steps. What's next if new back pain?"
   d. "You are an experienced personal injury attorney. Write a client update for a Florida personal injury case. The client wants to know what the next steps are and lets you know about new back pain he is having. Deliver your response as a client email."

3. Following up from Example 2, what should you do with the chatbot response to your query?
   a. Rate the response, regenerate if needed, copy it, edit, and revise for accuracy.
   b. Copy the response, skim it, and send it to client.
   c. Rewrite the entire response so it looks like it's in your words.
   d. Make sure it's grammatically correct and then send the letter.

4. After sending a letter to a client, she calls you to ask for the meaning of some words used in the letter. How can ChatGPT help with this problem?
   a. It can send the client a new letter.
   b. It can translate the letter.
   c. It can rewrite the letter for clarity if the user requests that specific direction.
   d. It can delete the letter and call the client to explain.

5. You are a solo practitioner. A potential client comes in for a consultation. He has an immigration issue, and you believe he is eligible for the Deferred Action for Childhood Arrivals (DACA) program. He says he is not sure if DACA is still legal but wants to know his options. What is the best query to put in an AI chatbot?
   a. "What are the most recent changes to the DACA program?"
   b. "Is this client eligible for DACA?"
   c. "What is DACA?"
   d. "Have there been any changes in the Immigration Reform Act?"

Explanations

1. (a.) Incorrect. ChatGPT must always be reviewed, edited, and checked for accuracy. **(b.) Correct.** It is best practice to start research with secondary sources. Then find the applicable case law and statutes. Draft the memo and use ChatGPT as a tool to revise. (c.) Incorrect. Sending a link to the statutes is not following the supervisor's instructions. (d.) Incorrect. The research and prediction requested required much more than finding an article.

2. (a.) Incorrect. Queries should be specific. The more information, the better. (b.) Incorrect. More information and directions would make this a better query. (c.) Incorrect. This answer is better but still not detailed enough. **(d.) Correct.** This is the best answer. It tells the chatbot what to do, the type of case, the jurisdiction, and information that needs to be analyzed and included in the letter. It even tells it the perspective to use and how to deliver the response.

3. **(a.) Correct.** This is the best answer. Rating the response trains ChatGPT to produce more accurate responses. Users must always review the response and revise as needed. (b.) Incorrect. Review the response before copying it to determine if it will need to be regenerated. A more thorough review should be done. (c.) Incorrect. This answer is not the best because it is not always necessary to rewrite the entire response if much of the output is accurate. Some parts may need a rewrite but not all. (d.) Incorrect. Grammar is not the only thing that should be edited.

4. (a.) Incorrect. ChatGPT will not send a letter to the client. Users must copy the response and send the letter themselves. (b.) Incorrect. It could translate the letter if it were in a different language but that is not what the facts state. Here, there are just a few legal words that the client does not understand. **(c.) Correct.** The user should input the original letter and ask the chatbot to rewrite the letter in laymen's terms so a client can understand better. (d.) Incorrect. ChatGPT cannot just delete the letter or call the client.

5. **(a.) Correct.** Generative AI can help lawyers find the changes in the law by allowing them to ask the question in one place. Of course, attorneys should check the answers for accuracy and never rely on AI for a final answer. (b.) Incorrect. Without more information in the query, ChatGPT cannot produce the most accurate response. It will likely tell the user a general answer about who is eligible for DACA. (c.) Incorrect. This answer choice is similar to the prior answer. With this query, only a general response is likely. (d.) Incorrect. This query may generate an informative response, but it won't be specific enough for what the attorney or researcher seeks.

CHAPTER 6

Understanding Statutes, Rules, and Regulations

Understanding the differences among primary sources is key to using them effectively. Knowing the sources that are needed and how to use them is important to the research process and a researcher should have a good understanding of types and applications of sources before using new technology or explaining the law. In this chapter, we'll go into detail on statutes, rules, and regulations, all different types of primary sources. As discussed in earlier chapters, statutes are laws made by legislative bodies. Rules and regulations are made by government agencies. Statutes are created at the state and federal levels. They are usually organized by subject matter and divided into chapters and sections using a unique numbering system. The federal government publishes the United States Code where all federal statutes and the text of the U.S. Constitution can be found.

States publish their statutes on state websites and in state code books. These publications may also include the language of the state constitution. Statutes are sometimes referred to as codes or statutory codes. Statutes and codes are interchangeable terms. When a rule is referred to as "codified" that means it is a law placed into permanent statute. Courts cannot change a statute, but they can interpret it. If a statute is challenged in court, the court may decide a statute is void for vagueness or unconstitutional if it is unclear or contradicts the state constitution. But these challenges have proven to be difficult.

Statutes are made with certain intentions in mind. They either prohibit conduct, permit conduct, or regulate conduct. But in doing that, Congress is not always clear. That is when courts, secondary sources, annotated codes, and other research tools can help with understanding a statute's meaning and intent. Some statutes address new issues that have not been addressed in common law. Some simply codify the common law rules.

Although government bodies publish their own codes, commercial companies may publish them as well. If a commercial publisher publishes the statutes without the government's permission, it is called an unofficial code. By contrast, official codes are published by the authority of the government. Because official codes come straight from the source, it is preferable to cite to official codes when available over unofficial codes. Keep in mind that sometimes it may be necessary to cite to unofficial codes if an amended statute has not yet been codified.

Published codes can be annotated or unannotated. Annotated codes contain statutory history, references to cases that interpret the statute, regulations that pertain to the statute, and secondary sources that discuss the statute. Both can be found on legal research engines.

RULES AND REGULATIONS

Congress makes laws but it also gives administrative agencies the responsibility and authority to enforce them. When a government agency makes policies in a specific area, those policies are called regulations or administrative rules. They create rules or regulations that implement the requirements of a statute.

The federal government publishes the Code of Federal Regulation (C.F.R.), which is an arrangement or codification of permanent federal regulations. It currently has 50 titles that cover broad areas of federal rules.

HOW IT WORKS

To begin researching a statute, start at the first page of the research platform. Find "Statutes" and click on the link (Figure 6.1). There, you can filter by jurisdiction. Find the statute by state and topic. Another way is to type the statute number into the search box, if you have been given the specific statute (Figure 6.2). Do the same for "Regulations" (Figure 6.3).

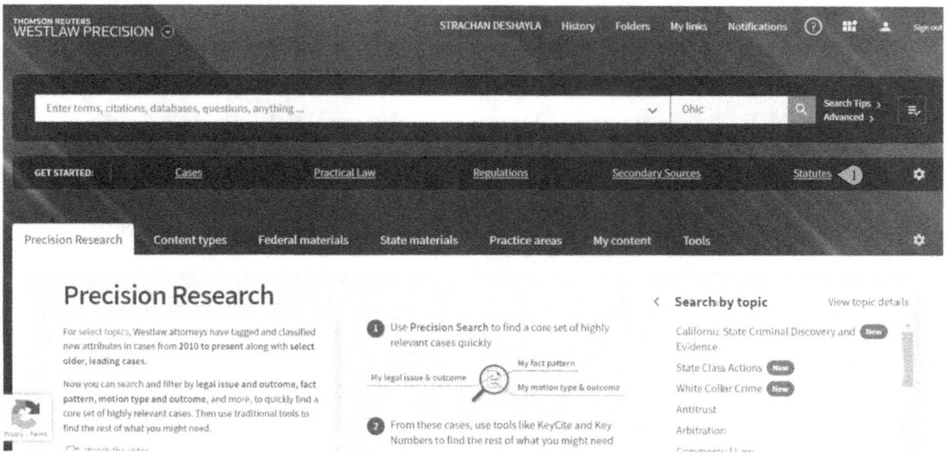

(1) Statutes

Figure 6.1 Statutes

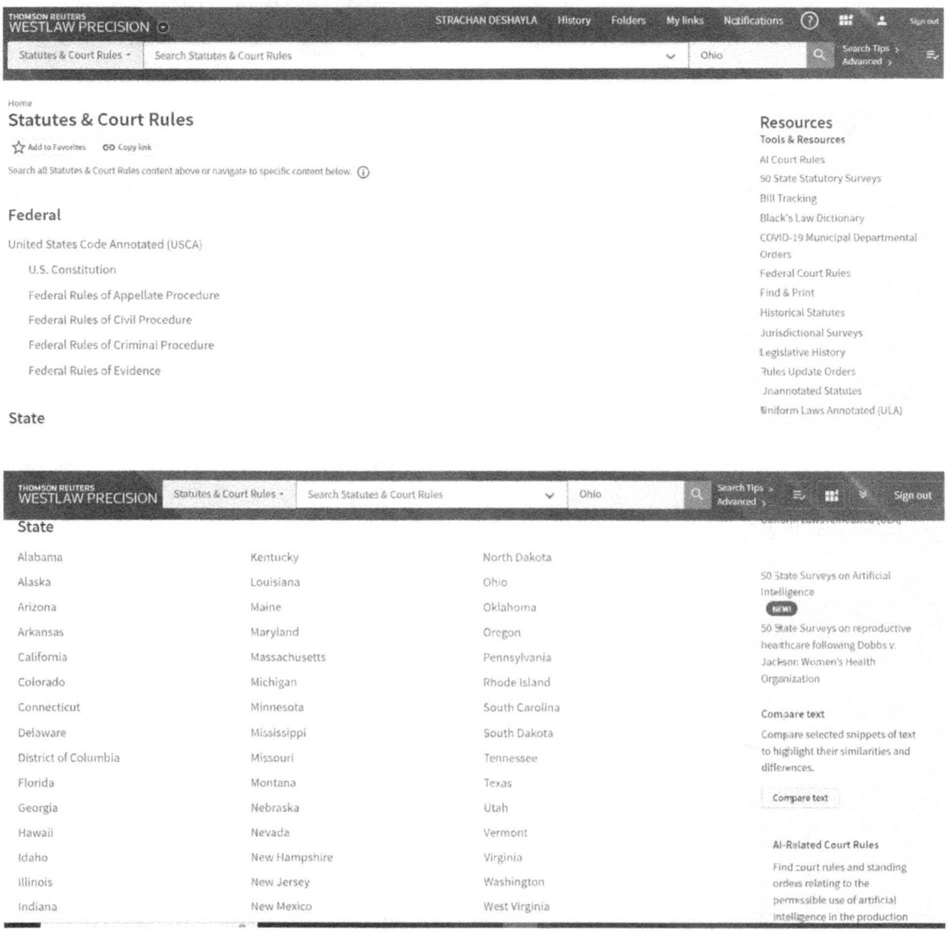

Figure 6.2 Find the Federal, State, or Topical Statutes

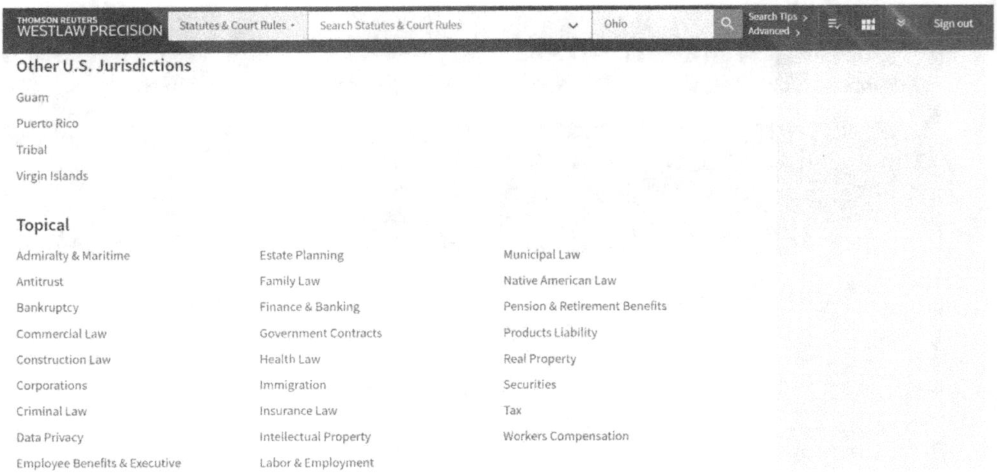

Figure 6.2 *Continued*

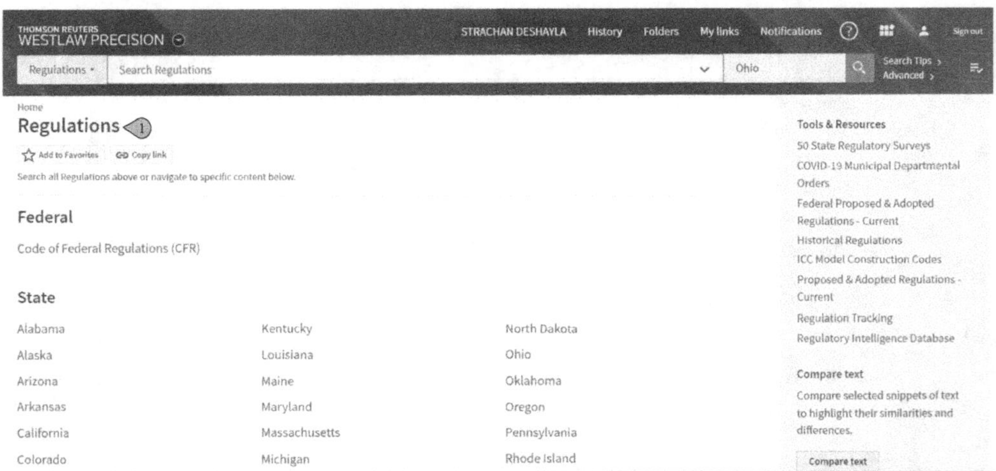

(1) Regulations

Figure 6.3 Follow the Same Steps to Find Regulations

Examples

1. You are on an internship in a family law firm. You have been given a research assignment from your supervising attorney and are asked to find out if there are any statutes in California that govern the grounds for dissolution of marriage. The client believes infidelity can be used as a ground. Where could you find the most accurate answer to this research question?
   a. Refer to a book you recently saw online about California family law.
   b. Ask a friend who went through a divorce what his lawyer said.
   c. Search statutes in a legal research engine, filter to California, family code, find Division 6 on nullity, dissolution, and legal separation, then click on Chapter 2 to see the grounds for legal separation.

   d. Search it up on Google, click on the California statutes site, and find it from there.

2. On a legal research assignment, you are asked to find the federal law that regulates the president's compensation. Where should you look first to find the most accurate information?
   a. Search for federal regulations in a legal research engine. Find Title 3, Chapter 2 of the United States Code Annotated. Standards of Conduct -> Compensation of the President.
   b. Ask AI to find the information and then cite to AI in your answer.
   c. Check the White House website.
   d. Consult a popular blog about government affairs.

3. When doing research for the upcoming open memo, you find a statute that you believe applies to your case. The language is not very clear, but it seems like it prohibits certain conduct. What is the best way to get a clear understanding of the statute?
   a. Read the statute over and over again to gain clarity.
   b. Ask your friends and family to read it and see what they think.
   c. Find the physical statute book in the law library and look up its history.
   d. On an online legal research engine, look at secondary sources citing the statute, as well as regulations and case law pertaining to it.

4. During your research on flight safety, you find a Federal Aviation Administration regulation on operating requirements. There are some interesting annotations in the U.S.C.A. (United States Code Annotated), an unofficial code mirroring the U.S.C. (United States Code). Which should you cite?
   a. Cite to either one.
   b. Always cite to the official code.
   c. Cite to both.
   d. Cite the most interesting code, whether official or not, whichever is more persuasive.

Explanations

1. (a.) Incorrect. The book may be helpful as a secondary source for background knowledge but may not have the most up-to-date information. (b.) Incorrect. A friend may not accurately convey the information they received from their attorney. The information may also not be up to date. **(c.) Correct.** Finding the proper statute on a legal research engine will give you the most recent version of the statute, exact wording, proper citation information, and legislative history. This information is likely what your supervisor is looking to receive. (d.) Incorrect. While Google can be helpful and point you in the right direction, it is best to use

proper legal research engines to perform legal research. This choice is not the best answer.

2. **(a.) Correct.** For federal regulations, the U.S. Code or C.F.R. is the best place to find official regulations enforcing federal statutes. (b.) Incorrect. AI may give you good background knowledge, but it may not have the most recent information or accurate citations. So, it is best to check the original source. (c.) Incorrect. The White House website may certainly have this information within linked documents, but the website is not a law, which is what you were asked to find. (d.) Incorrect. For the same reasons that (c.) is incorrect, the blog may have the correct law mentioned but is not the type of source your professor is looking for on this assignment.

3. (a.) Incorrect. No matter how many times you read it, the words remain the same. So, that will not help clear things up. (b.) Incorrect. It could be helpful to get other opinions but that is not a true or official way to get the meaning of the statute. (c.) Incorrect. If you can make your way to the law library near you, the physical statute book can help. It contains legislative history, but it may not have the most up-to-date information. **(d.) Correct.** Secondary sources, cases, and regulations can fill gaps and help you understand how courts interpret the statute. Legislative intent and legislative history can also be found in these sources.

4. (a.) Incorrect. If there is an official code to cite, it is best to cite the main source. **(b). Correct.** This is the best answer. Cite to the official code because it is the primary source, without comments or annotations from a commercial publisher. (c). Incorrect. While you could cite to both, it is best to cite to the official code when possible. The unofficial code could only be persuasive. (d.) Incorrect. For the same reasons, the official code is the best one to cite because it is the main and primary source. It is also fine to cite to both, understanding the official code is the binding, primary source regardless of how interesting the unofficial code may be.

CHAPTER 7

Using Good Law

GOOD LAW VERSUS BAD LAW

Now that you have researched and found cases, statutes, and regulations, it is time to make sure they are good law. The term "good law" means the case is still valid, up to date, and has not been overruled by a higher court. To keep your research up to date and relevant, it is critically important to filter all the primary sources you find to only include good law in your research. Statutes can be held unconstitutional, be amended or repealed, or even made obsolete by changes in the law. If the legal decision is no longer valid, then it cannot be used as a basis for legal arguments. You want to avoid "bad law" in your online research.

How do you determine if you have identified good law?

- Check the history
- Check subsequent citations
- Check the citator report

Identify where your issuing court is situated in the court system. Is it a state or federal court? Then review the subsequent appellate history and cases from relevant courts to ensure nothing has undermined or overturned your citation. Most important, use the relevant online tools to check your law.

Both Westlaw and Lexis have specific tools to check the status of these primary sources. Westlaw's tool is called KeyCite. On Lexis, the citator tool is called Shepard's. Be sure to KeyCite or Shepardize cases, statutes, and regulations before citing them. You don't want your supervising attorney, opposing counsel, or the judge pointing out that the law you relied on is no longer valid.

For statutes and regulations, check the currentness and versions by clicking on "Currentness and History" in the legal research engine. Red flags or signals on a case or law mean the case has been invalidated at least in part and is not good law (Figure 7.1). Yellow flags or signals mean another court has criticized, distinguished, or otherwise disagreed with a case on an issue (Figure 7.2). That means that case might not be as persuasive as another.

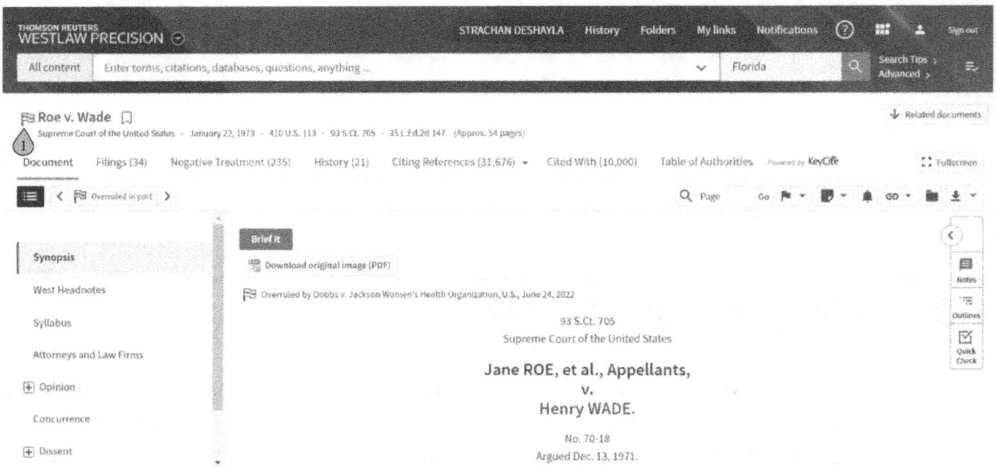

1 Red flag

Figure 7.1 Red Flag

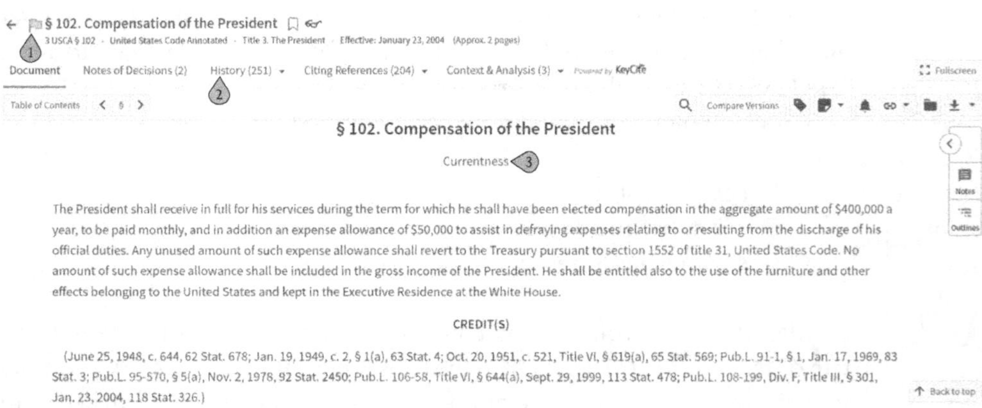

1 Yellow flag 2 Historu 3 Currentness

Figure 7.2 Yellow Flag

HOW IT WORKS

When looking at a case in the legal research engine, look for the flag in the top left corner next to the case name. Click on it. Then, you can see how other courts or the same court treated the decision. There will usually be a list of cases where the court followed the case, declined to follow the case, distinguished the case, or overruled it. The depth of treatment is also shown. That is the amount the case was discussed within the case that cited it. "Citing References" shows cases and secondary sources that have cited the case.

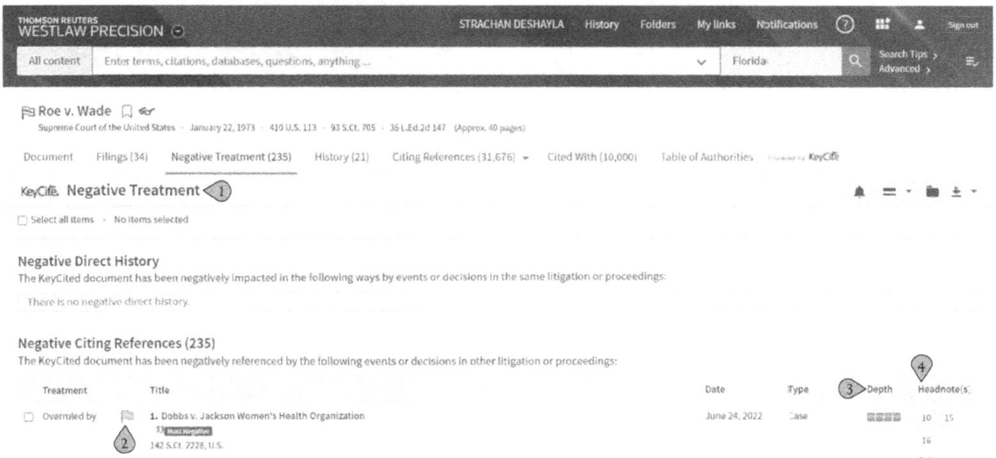

1 Negative treatment 2 Dobbs case with yellow flag 3 Depth 3 Headnotes

Figure 7.3 Exploring Negative Treatment

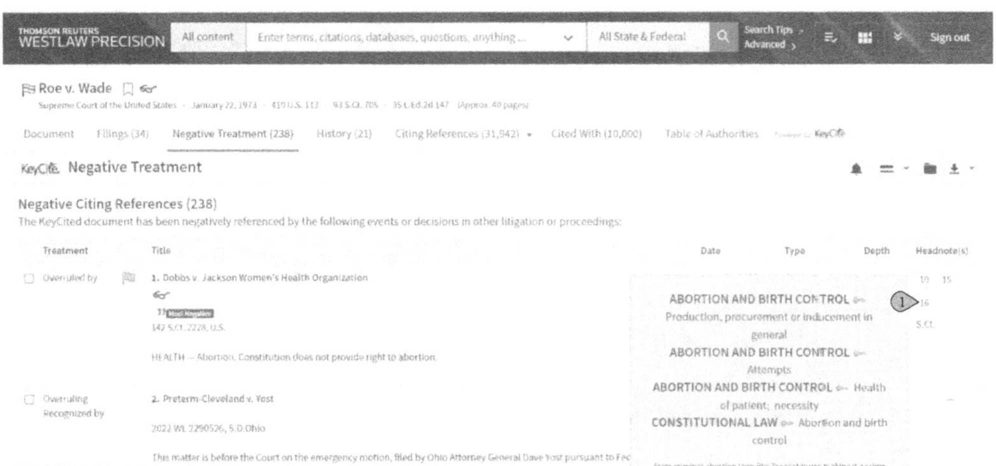

1 Headnote 16 2 Popout

Figure 7.4 Exploring Headnotes

7. Using Good Law

Sherpard's on Lexis+ looks similar to Westlaw. In Lexis, there will be a similar sign (red stop sign instead of a flag) in the upper left corner next to the case name (Figure 7.5). Click on the red stop sign. It will show a graph of negative treatment by U.S. circuit as well list each case that treated the case negatively (Figures 7.6 and 7.7).

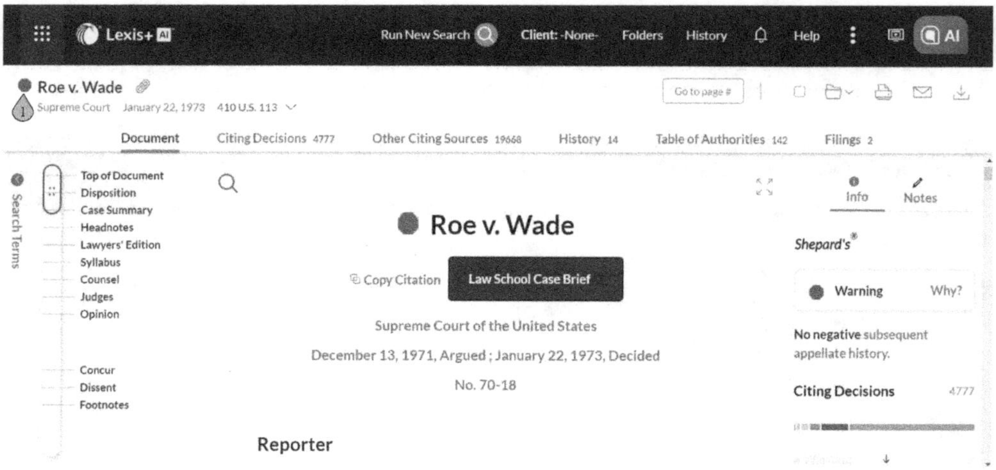

1 Red stop sign

Figure 7.5 Red Stop Sign

Figure 7.6 Graph of Negative Treatment

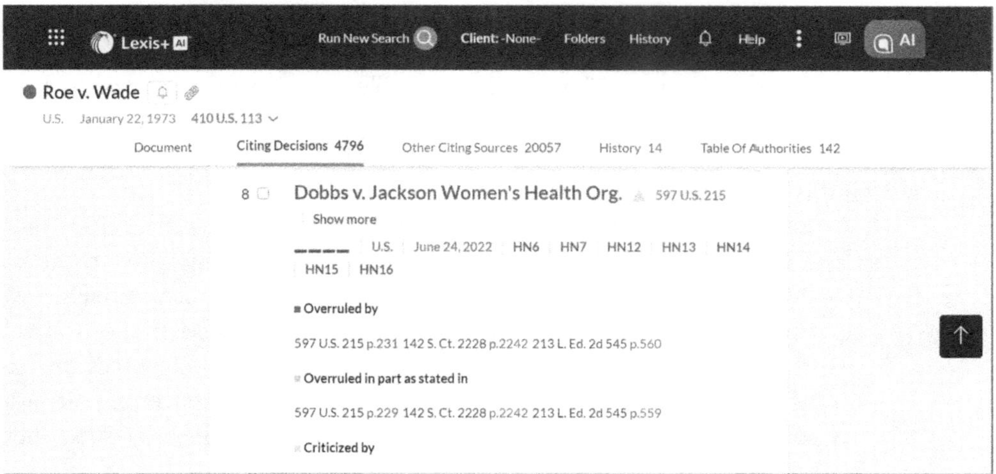

Figure 7.7 Individual Case of Negative Treatment

There are many helpful symbols in both Westlaw and Lexis that you should familiarize yourself with to make your legal research as efficient as possible. Let's explore some of these symbols.

Westlaw Status Flags

Red—The case is no longer good law.

Red stripe—The case was overruled in part, or on at least one issue. This is no longer good law on that point, but it may be good on others.

Yellow—The case has negative treatment on at least one issue but has not been reversed or overruled.

Blue-striped—The case has a pending appeal to the U.S. Court of Appeals or U.S. Supreme Court.

Orange circle around an exclamation mark—The case has a risk of being overruled because it relies on an invalid prior decision on at least one issue, therefore the case is at risk of being overruled itself.

Green—The case is good law and has no negative treatment.

Lexis Status Signals

Red stop sign—The case was overruled or superseded on at least one issue.

Orange square around a Q—The case's validity is in question by citing references or history. There is treatment that questions the precedential value or continuing validity of the case because of intervening circumstances, including judicial or legislative overruling as mentioned in the citing reference.

Yellow triangle—The case has possible negative treatment on at least one issue.

Green diamond around a plus sign—The case has positive treatment and is good law.

Blue circle around an A—The case has been cited in a neutral manner. Cases have assigned some analysis that is not considered positive or negative. It has only been explained but not treated negatively or positively.

Blue circle around an I—The case has been cited by secondary sources that do not have history or treatment analysis. So, citing references or history is available but there is no treatment because the references are secondary sources, which cannot be overruled or treated negatively because they are not law.

When finding that a case has been overruled, the researcher cannot use this case for the issue that it was overturned and will no longer be binding or persuasive. When a case has a yellow flag, the researcher should review the reason for the negative treatment but can still cite to the case because it has not been overturned. However, the case should be carefully read to see exactly what the court said. If the court distinguished the case with a case that is factually similar to your case, then it may not be a good idea to cite to the case after all. That is because the current court may actually be persuaded to take the same view as that distinguished case and rule against your client. Online citators are still fallible and may provide you with something that is no longer good law. It is best practice to check another citator and critically read the case to validate the status of the law. The court has discretion to reprimand or even sanction attorneys who try to rely on invalid law or misstate the law in bad faith. Citing bad law could also do harm to an attorney's reputation, causing judges to no longer find them credible. It can also be an ethics violation depending on the rules of the state bar. That is all in addition to the damage it does to the client's case and the law firm's reputation. So, knowing how to filter all your research to only ever use good law is extremely important for your future as a lawyer.

EXAMPLES

Examples

1. A client comes to you about a personal injury matter in Tennessee. She slipped and fell at an acquaintance's apartment and wants to know if she can recover from the acquaintance or the landlord. After reviewing cases for several hours, you come across a case that is very similar and the court found the landlord liable. The case has a red flag in Westlaw. What steps should you take now?

a. Use the case because the red flag is probably a mistake.
b. Ignore the red flag. As long as it's primary authority, the court won't care.
c. Click on the flag to review the case that overruled it and determine the issues that were overruled. Do not cite the case if overruled on the landlord liability issue.
d. Check if it was cited before. If so, then use it.

2. On a research assignment, there are a few cases provided to the class that may help answer the legal question about easement rights for cable companies. They all seem to be on point with the easement issue. One has a yellow flag at the top. The others have green signals. You are asked which cases you should use in a memo. Can you use the case with the yellow flag?
   a. Maybe. It depends on the reason for the negative treatment and if it was regarding the easement issue.
   b. Yes, definitely. If cases were provided, they can be used regardless of the treatment.
   c. Probably. Yellow flags always mean the case is still good law.
   d. No.

3. As a certified legal intern or student attorney on a criminal case, you are set for a motion hearing. Defense counsel has filed a motion to suppress evidence due to constitutional violations. You have been preparing to oppose the motion for a month. You've found several controlling cases to support your position. The supervising attorney asks you to use the cases in your oral argument. When sitting in court, you review one of your best cases and see that it was overruled three days ago. The hearing is starting, and you panic. Should you still rely on the case?
   a. Yes. It was overturned so recently that it won't make a difference.
   b. Yes, if it was not overruled on the issue at hand.
   c. No. If it was overruled at all, it's a bad look in court.
   d. Yes. The court should already know about it and understand.

4. While reviewing an article on intellectual property law written by a well-known practitioner, you decide you want to cite it in an upcoming memo. Do you need to check if it is good law?
   a. Yes. Always update your sources.
   b. No, because this author is too cool to be overruled.
   c. It depends.
   d. No. Secondary sources cannot be good or bad law because they are not law at all.

EXPLANATIONS

Explanations

1. (a.) Incorrect. Never assume the citator is mistaken. Always check negative treatment before relying on a case. (b.) Incorrect. Courts very much care about relying on valid law. If an attorney uses invalid law, it could be an ethics violation, sanction, or reprimand. **(c.) Correct.** When you see a red flag, you must review the case and determine the issues that were overturned. It may still be good law on the issue at hand. If so, citing to the case is ok. If the case has been overruled on all issues or specifically your issue, do not cite to the case. (d.) Incorrect. Even if a case has been cited in previous cases or publications, that does not mean it is good law. The case may have been cited before being overturned.

2. **(a.) Correct.** Read the cases that distinguished or criticized the case you want to use. If they are only distinguishing it because the facts are not the same, and your case facts are closer to the original case's facts, then citing the case is fine. If the case is being distinguished or criticized due to a fact that is also present in your case, it may not be helpful to cite. (b.) Incorrect. Any case you plan to rely on should be critically read. Even if you were provided with cases from a professor or supervisor, a lawyer should always update the case to see if the law is still valid. This should also be practiced in law school. (c.) Incorrect. While a case with a yellow flag often is still good law, it is not always true. Reading the case is still required. (d.) Incorrect. This answer is too absolute. The case must be read, along with the negative treatment, to determine if it can be used.

3. (a.) Incorrect. It doesn't matter if a case was just recently overturned. If it is invalid, it cannot be cited. **(b.) Correct.** This is the best answer. If there is still any time to review the treatment to see which issue was overruled, do that. If it was not overruled on your issue, you should still rely on the case. If it was, do not mention the case. It is always important to update cases even on the day of court to avoid this type of panic. (c.) Incorrect. Just because a case has negative treatment or has been overturned on an issue does not necessarily make the whole case bad to use in the view of the court. Courts understand that cases can be superseded or overruled partially, leaving some good law within it. (d.) Incorrect. Even if you think the court has already read and updated the case, it still cannot be cited if it was reversed, overruled, or superseded on your issue. If it was cited in a memo submitted to the court previously, explain that you understand the case has since been overturned (if on your issue). Courts appreciate candor. It is best for you to acknowledge an updated case instead of a judge telling you that your main case is no good.

4. (a.) Incorrect. Always update sources but only primary sources. However, you should check primary sources cited within secondary sources for

their validity. (b.) Incorrect. Secondary sources are not law, so they cannot be overruled. The author's coolness is irrelevant. (c.) Incorrect. The only thing this answer depends on is if it is actually a primary source, which it is not. **(d.) Correct.** This is the best answer. As mentioned, only primary sources are overruled or treated positively or negatively. Secondary sources are not law and are not treated as such. These sources could rely on outdated law though, so they must be checked for accuracy and currentness.

CHAPTER 8

Defining and Refining a Research Question

When preparing an objective memo or persuasive motion or brief, it is important to not only define your research question but also to refine it. Define it by understanding and clarifying exactly what the legal question is. Once more facts are discovered, it may be necessary to refine the question by making it more specific. To define the question, first, understand the area of law specific to your research. Is it Torts, Contracts, Property, Criminal, or a mix of areas? Next, determine how many issues need to be addressed. If there are three elements to a cause of action, there should be three separate legal questions that need to be answered. Then, refine the research questions by asking yourself the narrow legal question or questions that need to be answered. A client's legal question typically turns on the facts. So, you must have a comprehensive understanding of the facts before you begin researching.

Sometimes you will be given a specific question to research. Other times you may be given a broad area to research and need to narrow it down to a specific question or questions in order to get a good understanding and answer(s). To do that, review the facts you have and think about what types of rules may apply. It could be a statute or case law, or both. The best, most specific legal questions include the facts from the client's case.

In legal research class, you may have been asked to write a question presented. To write a question presented, you must know the jurisdiction's law, the question that needs to be decided, when certain facts are present. For example, a question presented could be, "Under Nevada law, can a pedestrian carry an open container of alcohol on the street if it is in a plastic cup?" A well-drafted research question is as important as finding the right answer.

The better the question, the more accurate the answer. Remember that the question should not be too broad or too narrow. If too broad, it will yield an overwhelming number of results. If too narrow, it may not yield any results. Find the sweet spot that will produce the most helpful results.

HOW IT WORKS

In your legal research class, you will get a fact pattern of a fictional client's case from your professor. Then, if not given a specific legal question, or given a broad legal question, you need to review the facts and define the legal question by finding the appropriate area of law and whether statutes or case law apply. Get even more specific once you understand the language of the law, how courts have treated similar situations, and what facts the case turns on.

In practice, clients will explain their problem and ask if they have a case. Supervising attorneys may ask junior attorneys a broad question like, "What remedies are available to concert goers who are hurt on the premises?" It will be up to you to break this question down into narrower research questions. For example, you may want to know if the client signed a liability release, the specific jurisdiction, and if the client contributed to the injury in any way. Think about the areas of law that could apply and determine the legal standards. With the facts presented, issues spotted, and knowledge of the law, you should be able to begin crafting your legal questions.

When the fact pattern does not immediately present a legal question or it is harder to identify the law that would apply, think about the facts more critically. Consider the location, the relationship of the parties involved, the conduct, injuries, mental state, age, etc. Define a legal question from the facts and the applicable law should flow from there.

Let's say a potential client starts telling you about a situation she was in where she believes she was wronged but is not sure if there is a case or any remedy available. She said her son was hurt playing soccer at a friend's house. She is not sure where or how exactly the injury happened, but she paid expensive medical bills. There are many questions to ask in order to determine if there is any liability. Where exactly was the soccer game? Was it on the friend's property? How old were the children playing? What were the injuries? Were other parents or adults around? Were there any other witnesses? Were any cameras anywhere? What was the son doing at the time of the injury? When did this event occur? By asking these questions, you can tell if there may be any liability on the part of a property owner or parental neglect. Knowing when the event occurred will help with determining if the injury is within the statute of limitations. The age of the children will give some guidance about the level of supervision that should have been given. Knowing if his own conduct contributed to or caused the injury could determine if there is a proper negligence claim or defenses.

EXAMPLES

Examples

1. In the facts of your case, your client slipped on an unknown liquid at an Indiana concert venue and fell. She hurt her hip and ankle. She comes to your firm to see if she can sue the venue for having a wet floor and causing her injuries even though she signed a liability release when she bought the concert ticket. What do you do first?
   a. Ask a colleague what to do because he had a case like this once.
   b. Identify the area of law and define the legal question.
   c. Call the venue to see what really happened.
   d. Start writing the memo based on your initial thoughts.

2. Based on the facts from the previous Example, what would be the best legal question(s)?
   a. Can the client prevail in this case?
   b. Will the client win a negligence suit against the venue?
   c. Under Indiana law, does a venue have a duty of care to a plaintiff attending an event there? Does a venue breach that duty when allowing a liquid to remain on the floor and a plaintiff slips and falls?
   d. Does the liability release absolve the venue of any responsibility for any and all negligence?

3. Based on the facts from the first Example, what areas of law would apply?
   a. Criminal and Property law
   b. Evidence law
   c. Constitutional law
   d. Torts and Contracts law

EXPLANATIONS

Explanations

1. (a.) Incorrect. Asking a colleague may be helpful to start, but each case is unique and the law could have been updated since his last case. It is best to still do your own research first. **(b.) Correct.** After thoroughly reviewing the facts, decide what area or areas of law apply and define the legal questions. It may be Contracts, Torts, or both. The questions may need to be broken down by the elements of negligence and the legal standard for enforceable liability releases in the jurisdiction must be determined. (c.) Incorrect. Calling or visiting the venue could happen in the discovery stage when you are gathering evidence, but that is not the first step of the research process. (d.) Incorrect. It may help to jot down the statement of facts as you know them, but make sure you understand the question and law before writing the meat of the memo.

2. (a.) Incorrect. This question is too broad and vague. It leads to too many follow-up questions. (b.) Incorrect. This question is better because it at least points to an area of law but is still too broad. **(c.) Correct.** This answer is the best choice. The questions mention a jurisdiction and case facts and specify elements of the claim. (d.) Incorrect. Just as the other incorrect answer choices, this question also needs to be more specific.
3. (a.) Incorrect. Criminal law would include a crime being committed against a person or property. In these facts, no crime is stated. So, it is a civil case. (b.) Incorrect. The rules of evidence are typically triggered by trial. These facts seem to start at the beginning of an incident and do not yet discuss statements or items to be used in trial. (c.) Incorrect. Constitutional law issues are triggered by circumstances that arise under the constitution. We do not have that in this scenario. **(d.) Correct.** Slip and fall claims fall under Torts. Someone was harmed likely because of another party's lack of care. But the facts also mention a liability release, which could fall under Contract law.

CHAPTER 9

Filter and Search

We have discussed how to do simple searches during the planning phase and with AI tools. But what is the best way to perform the search? Could there be a special way to organize the words in the search box to get optimal results? Once you have defined and refined the research question, begin searching with specific search terms that might return the most useful results. These searches can be done via a plain-language search likened to those done on any internet search engine, as we discussed earlier, but there are also more particular ways of searching on online legal research engines to make your research as quick and effective as possible.

Some engines allow for the use of "boolean connectors" or "connectors." This method of searching connects certain words to each other in order to be found together or within the same sentence or paragraph of a source, rather than looking for the words anywhere within a source. For example, you could use a connector such as "AND" in a search box to find the words "book" and "report" together, by typing "book AND report." Without the "AND," the search engine would look for those words separately and might return documents that only contain one word or the other. "OR" can be used similarly.

Other connector commands can be used to make your search even more specific. Instead of just looking for a document that contains both words, you might want to find both words within the same paragraph. In this case, "book/p report" would return results with the words within the same paragraph. To get even more specific, "book/s report" would return results of the words "book report" within the same sentence.

Another way to use connectors would be to search within numerical proximity of certain words, exclude terms, or expand terms. For example, "book/3 report" returns results of the word "book" within three words of "report." If you wanted to search for documents related to books but did not want to include ones related to reports, you could search "book but not report." To expand terms, type an exclamation point after a word and that will generate results for different variations of a word. For example, "book!" will return results for books, booking, booked, bookie, etc. When a search uses these specific words or symbols, it is called a Boolean search. It helps refine results for a more precise search.

It is highly useful to learn these connectors for your online legal research. We have seen how defining and refining the legal question results in a specific search with a lot of relevant parts, so it's important for you to know how to compose an online search with multiple parts. If you have to search each aspect of your case separately and comb through lots of examples that are only tangentially relevant, you'll lose a lot of valuable time and may miss the most relevant cases.

CONNECTORS*

General

Root expander (!)
Use to search for words with multiple endings. For example, enter "object!" to retrieve "object," "objected," "objection," and "objecting."

Universal character (*)
Use to search for words with variable characters. For example, enter "withdr*w" to retrieve "withdraw" and "withdrew."

Search exactly as typed (#)
Use to search for a word exactly as you entered it, use the pound symbol (#). For example, enter "#damage" to retrieve "damage" but not "damages."

Grammatical

/p
Search terms must appear in the same paragraph (ex: hearsay/p utterance).

* See Appendix B and Appendix C for more comprehensive lists of Lexis and Westlaw search terms and connectors.

+p
The first search term must precede the second term in the same paragraph (ex: ti(burke +p burke)).

/s
Search terms must appear in the same sentence (ex: design/s defect).

+s
The first search term must precede the second term in the same sentence (ex: attorney +s fee).

Numerical

/n
Search terms must appear within "n" terms of each other, where "n" is a number from 1 to 255 (ex: personal/3 jurisdiction).

+n
The first search term must precede the second term by "n" terms, where "n" is a number from 1 to 255 (ex: capital +3 gain).

BUT NOT connector (%)
You can exclude documents that contain certain terms by using the BUT NOT connector (%). Westlaw excludes everything that follows the BUT NOT connector in your search. For example, the query "tax taxation % income/3 tax taxation" retrieves any document that contains the terms "tax" or "taxation," but excludes documents where those terms appear within three words of "income."

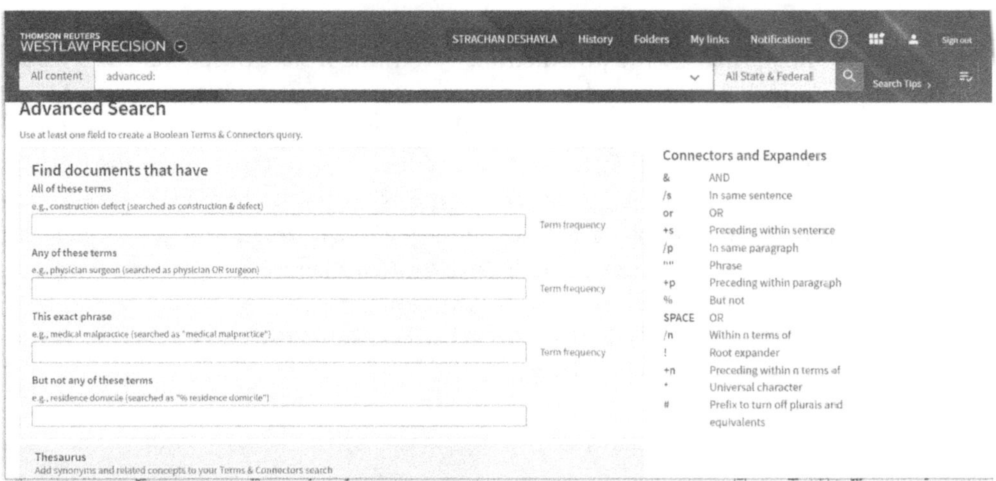

Figure 9.1 Connectors in the Advanced Search Tab on Westlaw Under Search Tips

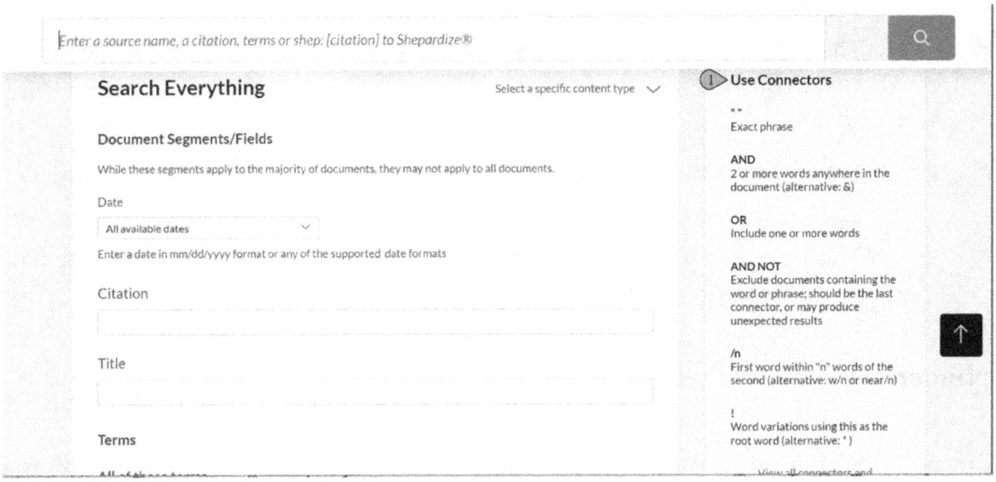

1 Use connectors

Figure 9.2 Connectors on Lexis+ with Advanced Search

FILTERING

As discussed previously, before you begin to type in search terms, it is best to filter so you can get the best, most specific results. Once you have your research plan with an articulated legal question and a list of search terms, it is time to engage in pre-search filtering. Narrowing a search with filters assists with finding binding primary authority. Like prompt engineering for the best AI responses, search results can be manipulated by how much you filter information before searching.

First, filter by the jurisdiction. Determine if state or federal cases would be most helpful and filter by the state or federal circuit, or both. If you somehow are unsure of your jurisdiction or want a very broad selection of materials, select "All State" and "All Federal." Next, think about the types of sources you are looking for. What type of materials or content would you like to review? Only cases and statutes? Or will other sources be helpful? Advanced search filters in both Lexis and Westlaw offer even more options, such as filtering by case facts and cause of action.

See Westlaw "Precision Filters" for specific attributes you can use to filter your search (Figure 9.3).

9. Filter and Search

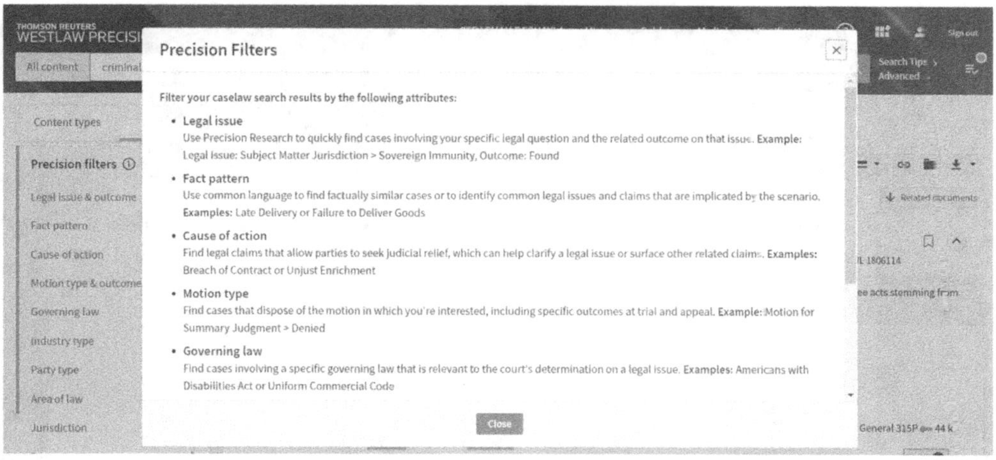

Figure 9.3 Precision Filters

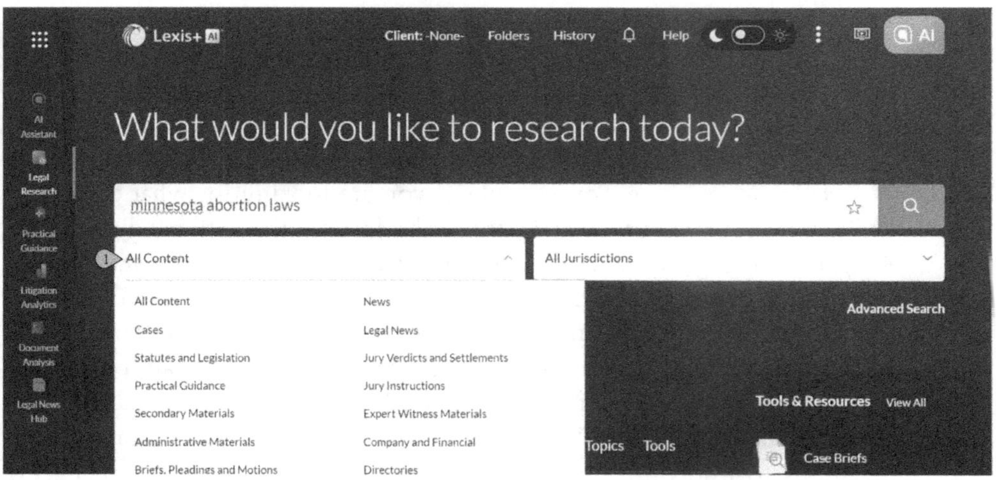

(1) All content

Figure 9.4 All Content

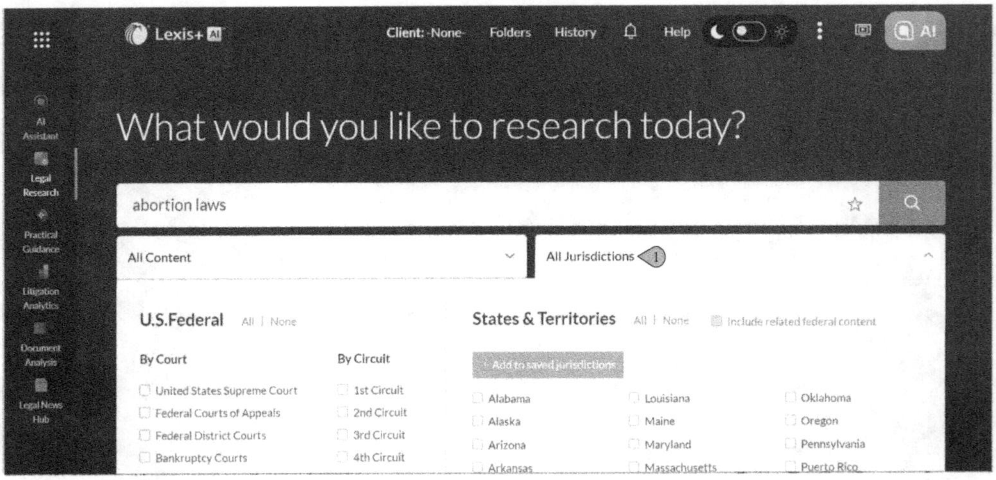

(1) All jurisdictions

Figure 9.5 All Jurisdictions

Let's walk through the search process, from the simplest first steps covered in Chapter 2 up to the more advanced and specific techniques introduced here. The easiest way to begin a search, you'll remember, is to do a plain-language search in the search bar to get the most helpful authority. Use terms found in secondary authority ("terms of art") and include key facts from your case. For example, if you are looking for what constitutes "outrageous conduct" in an intentional infliction of emotional distress case, type in outrageous conduct when approaching minors. Connect the term of art and facts by searching "outrageous conduct/5 minors." This search will produce cases and materials with the terms within five words of the facts mentioned. After running a basic search, you may have an overwhelming number of results. It is possible to filter by date range, reported cases, party name, judges, etc. There is also an option to search within results that will narrow down the results to particular cases that involve another set of terms you include. Some research engines will offer their own set of filters, such as Westlaw's Precision Filters. These allow you to filter by fact patterns, areas of law, legal issue, motion type, and others. Multiple filters can also be combined.

When doing plain-language searches, be thoughtful in your wording. Some words have common synonyms in case law. For example, a liability release could also be known as a waiver or exculpatory clause. Think of the synonyms that could be used in your case and search for those words too. A plain language search using a connector may be "reasonable person w/2 standard" or "reasonably prudent person." As you begin typing in the search bar, a dropbox will come down with suggestions. Putting quotation marks around the search term will narrow results to materials with those exact words in that order. And remember, connectors bring even more specificity to the results.

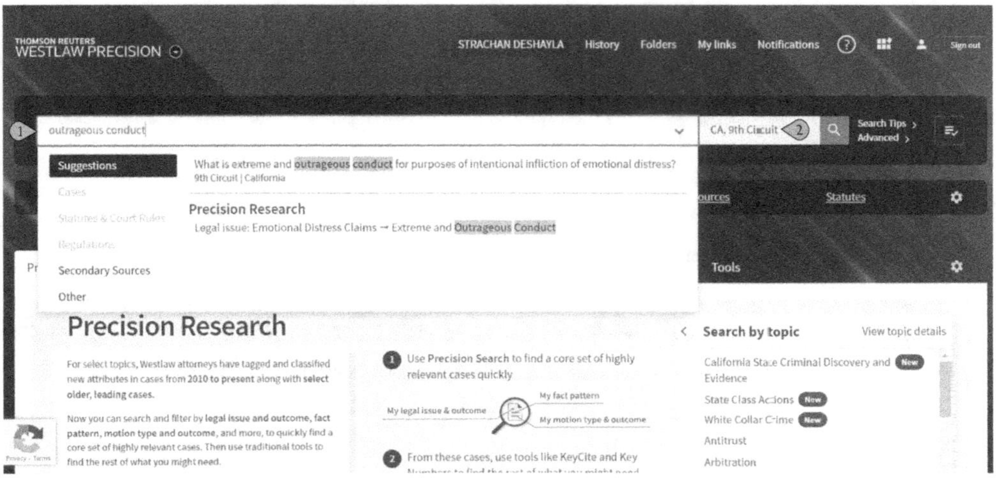

1 Search bar 2 CA, 9th Circuit filter

Figure 9.6 Search

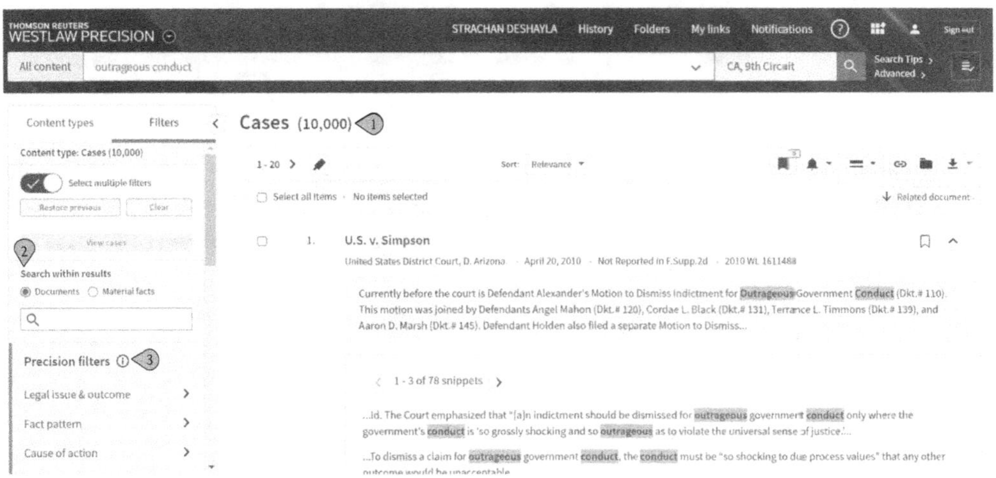

1 Cases (10,000) 2 Search within results 3 Precision filters

Figure 9.7 Search Results

9. Filter and Search

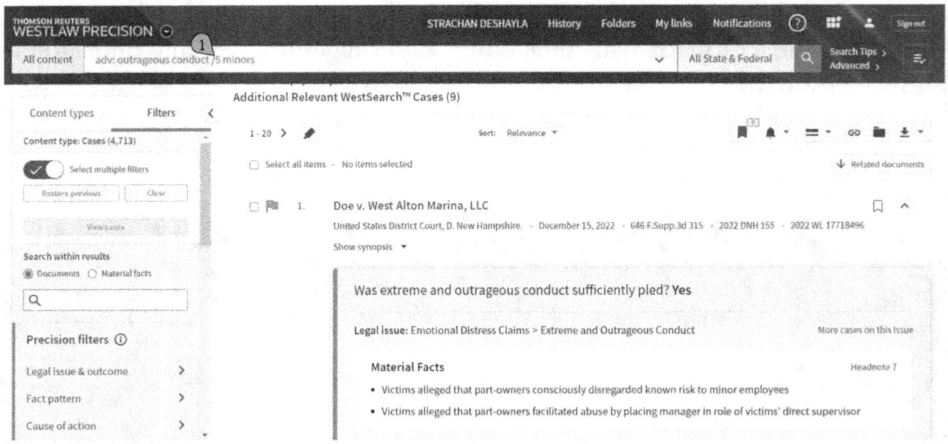

1 Search bar with connector

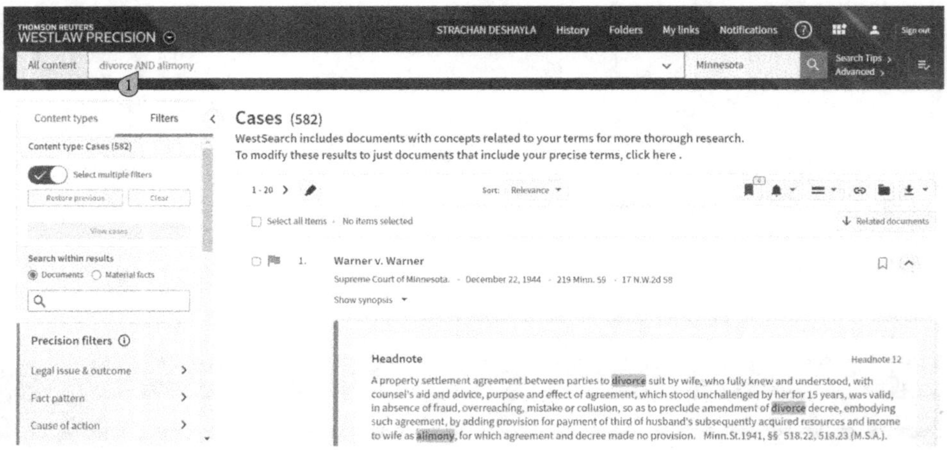

1 Connector

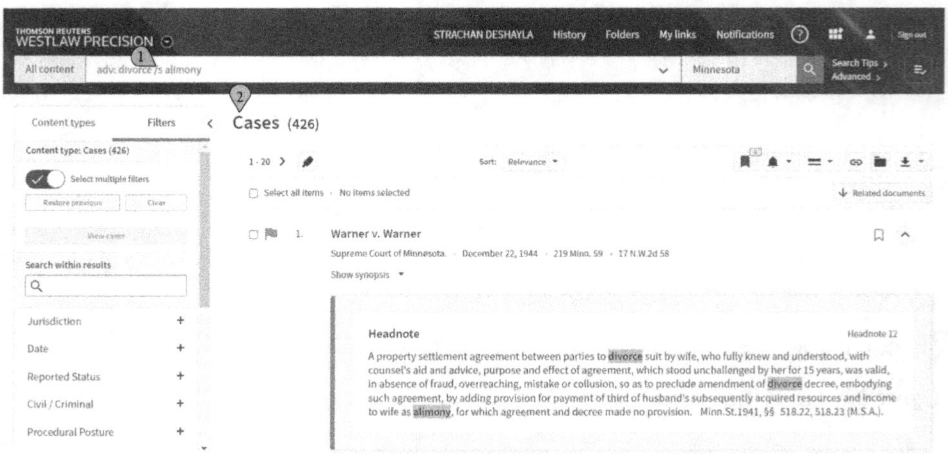

1 Connector 2 Cases with fewer results

Figure 9.8 Using Connectors

EXAMPLES

Examples

1. In Evidence class, you are tasked with determining if a statement used in court could be classified as an excited utterance and not be considered hearsay. You must use New York state law. What's the best way to search for this rule?
   a. Get the textbook and look up the federal rule and cases regarding the issue.
   b. Do a plain-language search for "excited utterance" in an online legal research engine after filtering to New York.
   c. Type in the question in a search bar.
   d. Visit the law library at a New York law school to get the state evidence rule.

2. You are given a fact pattern that involved the intentional tort of battery. The professor requires you to find similar cases where the court found a battery occurred. How would you begin the search?
   a. Use any applicable filters, search "battery tort" in the search bar. Then, narrow results by using connectors, other commercial filters, and case facts.
   b. Just type "battery" in the search bar.
   c. Find secondary sources that discuss battery.
   d. See what Wikipedia says about battery as a tort and then use terms from there on Westlaw.

3. Using the information in Example 2, which connectors could best be used to better this search?
   a. Tort, assault AND battery
   b. Batteries OR assault
   c. Battery! but not criminal/p intentional tort
   d. Criminal and tort battery/5 assault

EXPLANATIONS

Explanations

1. (a.) Incorrect. The class textbook will offer likely only the federal rules of evidence. The question calls for state law. **(b.) Correct.** The easiest and often most efficient way to begin a search is to do a plain-language search. But not before filtering to the correct jurisdiction. Here, the jurisdiction is New York so the search is done after filtering to that state. (c.) Incorrect. This answer is not specific enough. The location of the search bar and whether filters are used is not included. It is not clear if the search bar is even on a legal research platform. (d.) Incorrect. Visiting a state law library could help but it is not the most efficient way to search. Books may not be the most recent and may not even be available in some instances. An online legal research engine is best.

2. **(a.) Correct.** If you have the jurisdiction and case facts, you can narrow your search by including the jurisdiction. The commercial filters provided by Westlaw and Lexis could help you to narrow your search by the area of law and fact patterns. Connectors could also improve the search. (b.) Incorrect. Only typing the word "battery" would be too broad. Results would range from criminal battery to torts. (c.) Incorrect. Secondary sources are great, but the professor asked for cases. So, you can also filter to only be provided cases. That is the best place to begin because you are likely already familiar with the intentional tort of battery at this stage. (d.) Incorrect. Wikipedia and other online sources may not always be reliable. This is not the best answer.

3. (a.) Incorrect. The facts and question posed by the professor did not mention assault, so that term may muddy the waters. (b.) Incorrect. The same is true for the term batteries, which may mean something else, with assault and may not return the best results. **(c.) Correct.** Several connectors are used here to expand the word battery (battered, batteries, etc.), exclude the word criminal, and find the variation of battery within a paragraph of intentional tort. These combined connectors would likely return the best, most specific results. (d.) Incorrect. Again, we are only looking for the intentional tort of battery and not assault.

CHAPTER 10

Putting It All Together

Whew! That was a lot.

Online legal research can be tedious, but it does not have to be hard. With a good plan and the right tools, online legal research can be done very efficiently and effectively. Decide which legal research engine is preferred and works best for you. Learn to navigate that platform and take advantage of its best features. Use AI responsibly and only as allowed per school or professor policies.

Online legal research boils down to three main steps: Information gathering, law gathering, and updating. In the information gathering stage, you are getting the facts straight, learning the jurisdiction, and understanding the legal questions. In the law gathering stage, you are finding supporting legal sources (secondary and primary authority) to help your case. In the updating stage, you are making sure every law you have gathered is accurate and still valid.

The U.S. legal system is set up in tiers and relies heavily on precedent from previous decisions. Cases are the most-used primary source and are important in predicting the outcome of a legal issue. They are also important when persuading a court to rule in your favor. Use the most specific terms and words to define the legal question and find the best cases. These are the cases that are most relevant to your fact pattern, are preferably binding on your court, and if not binding are the most persuasive.

Secondary sources play a significant role in online legal research as well. They can provide an overview of the law in a specific area and can inspire creative arguments. Because most traditional secondary sources are explaining the law, commenting on the law, or making an argument about a specific area of the law, they may inspire or shape your argument or view as well. Do not overlook these sources when starting to research. But also, be cautious about certain sources that are less well vetted, such as blawgs or AI engines, and be sure to verify their information even more than other secondary sources.

Make a research plan to keep everything organized and tracked. Take good notes. Use synonyms, filters, and connectors when researching to find the most relevant cases without having to sift through piles of slightly related cases. Save relevant cases in online folders so you can quickly retrieve them.

When you see the same cases and statutes come up after hours and days of researching a variety of search terms and sources, you are done. But do not forget to update your sources using citators and updating tools on the legal research platform. Make your assessment of the case if producing an objective memo. Think of the most persuasive way to accurately present the law if producing a persuasive document. Now it is time to write.

But first, let's bring it all together using the hypothetical mentioned in Chapter 8. Remember the potential client whose son was injured playing soccer at a neighbor's house? Let's see how we will determine the legal question and answer it.

HYPOTHETICAL

Step 1:

Gather the information you have. In a law school setting you will only have the facts provided. In practice, you will be able to contact the client to gain more information. So, with the given facts we only know that the son was hurt at a friend's house while playing soccer. But let's say you found out more information. The injury actually happened at a park in the friend's neighborhood. They live in Florida and the children were all 14 years old. The child was accidentally hit pretty badly in the mouth and had to have major dental surgery. The accident happened about a month ago. There were no neighborhood cameras but there were others watching them play. One of the friend's parents was home. With this information, we can begin to form the legal question and begin some research.

Step 2:

Gather the law needed to answer the legal question. With these facts, we might ask legal questions such as, "Under Florida law, are parents responsible for injuries that happen to others under their supervision?" Or "Under Florida law, is a homeowners' association liable for injuries that happen in common areas?" You see, the legal question(s) can change upon learning new facts. You might even reword them to produce narrower results or more results as we discussed in previous chapters.

Next, pick a research engine to begin your research. We will use Westlaw for this example. Filter to the correct jurisdiction, which is Florida. Start with secondary sources.

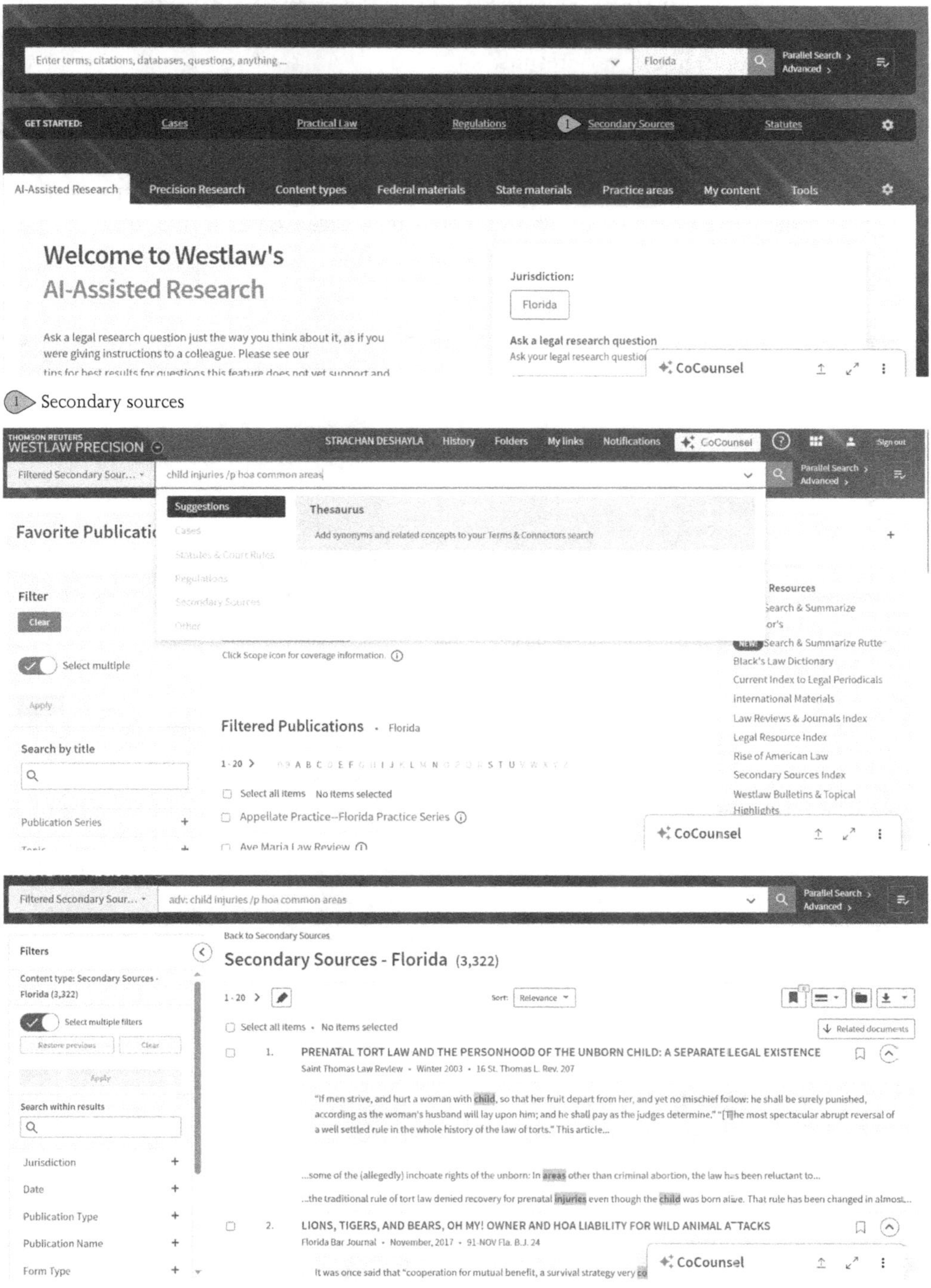

Figure 10.1 Start with Secondary Sources

The first search using a few terms and a connector produced more than 3,000 results. Change the terms or ask a specific question to get less results.

So, asking a question here yielded more results (as shown above in Figure 10.2). However, revising the search terms yielded only 525 results (as shown below in Figure 10.3). You see how the words, connectors, and phrases used can vary results.

Now, look through relevant secondary sources to see what the legal trends are and find primary sources. Next, let's search for primary sources directly assuming we did not find an on-point case within the secondary sources.

First, filter to jurisdiction (Figure 10.4). Then, use terms and connectors in the search bar. Remember that you can enter terms, questions, or citations. Let's start with terms (Figure 10.5).

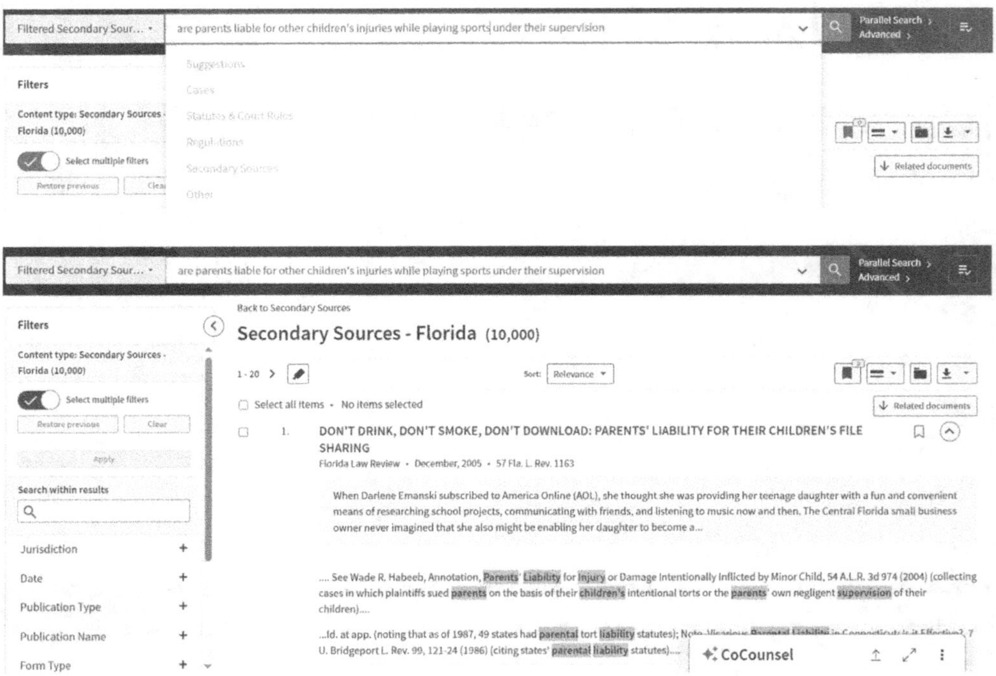

Figure 10.2 Narrow the Search

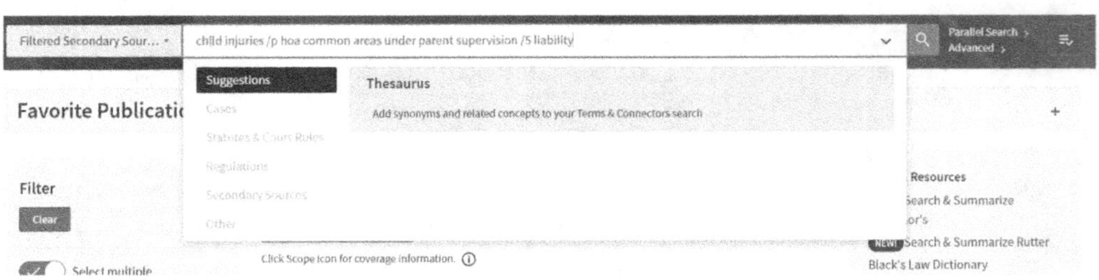

Figure 10.3 Continue to Narrow the Search

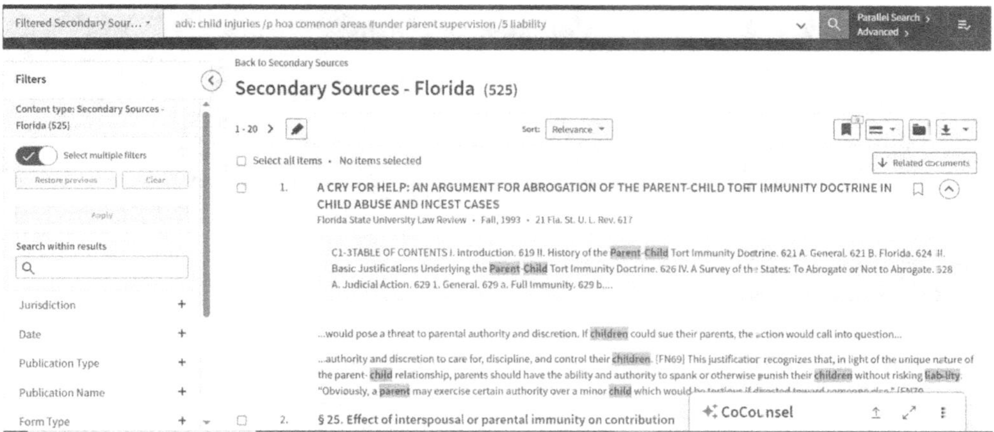

Figure 10.3 Continued

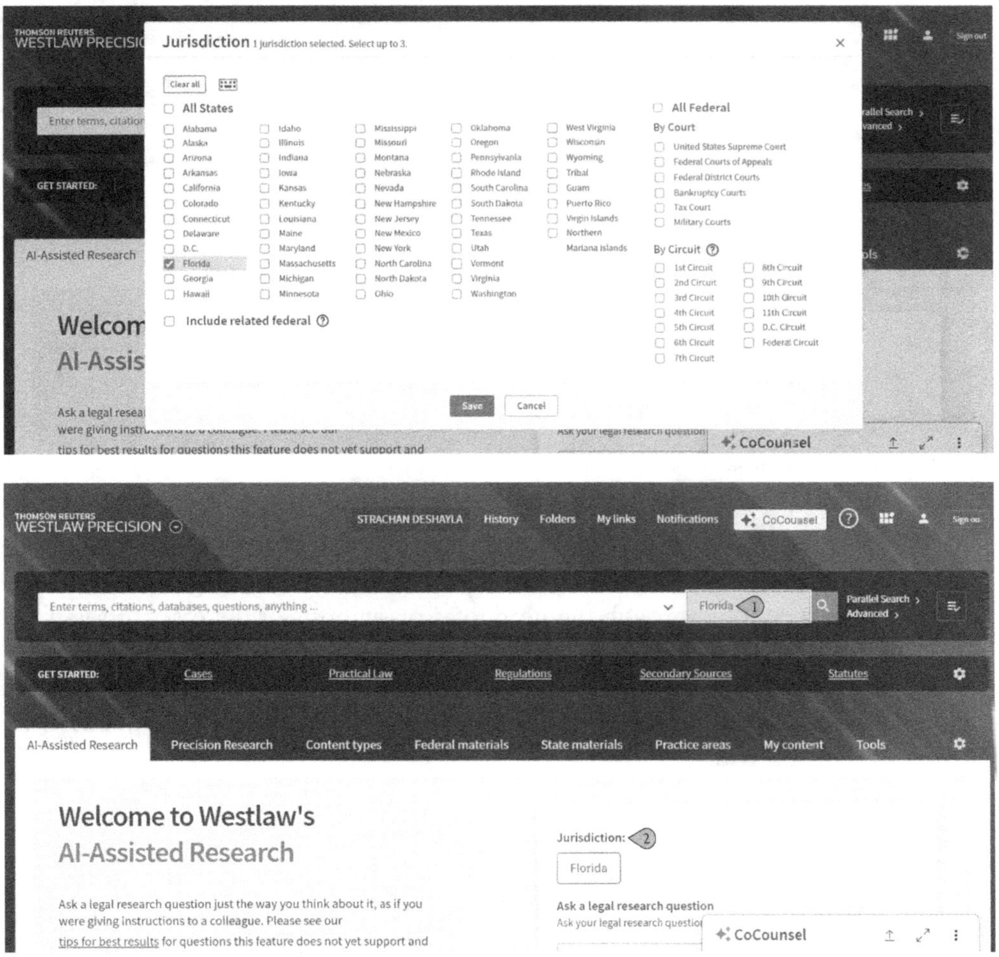

(1) Search bar (2) Jurisdiction

Figure 10.4 Filter to Jurisdiction

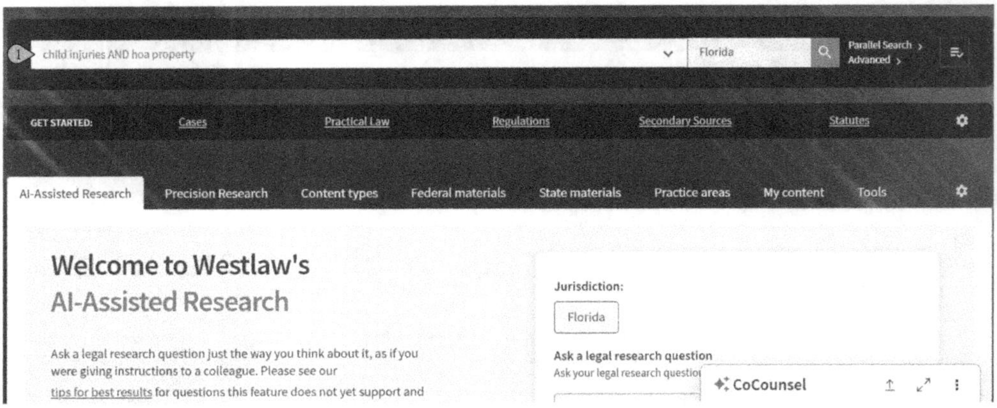

1 Search bar

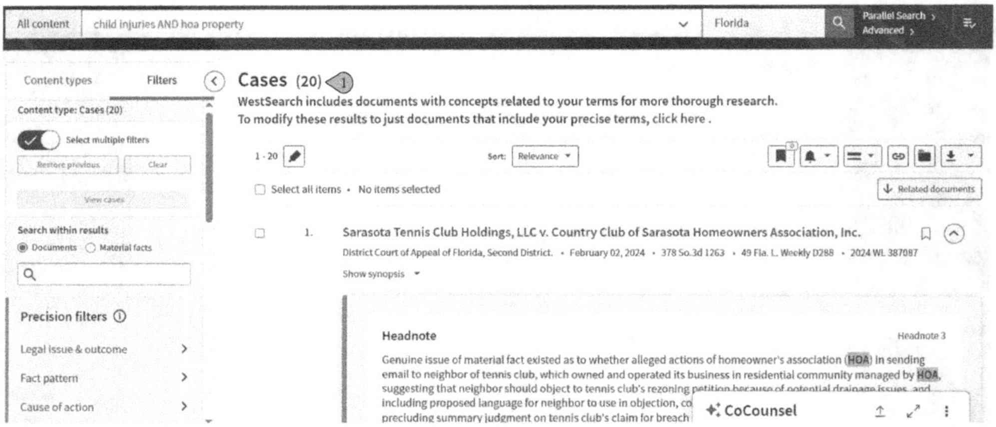

1 Cases (20)

Figure 10.5 Using Terms and Connectors

As you can see, these simple search terms with the "And" connector produced 20 cases that may be helpful in answering the legal questions. You can then look through the headnotes or synopsis of the cases to see if the case applies. Let's try inputting one of the legal questions.

Searching the question yielded just one more result than the search terms but the results are more specific. Let's try the other legal question we came up with.

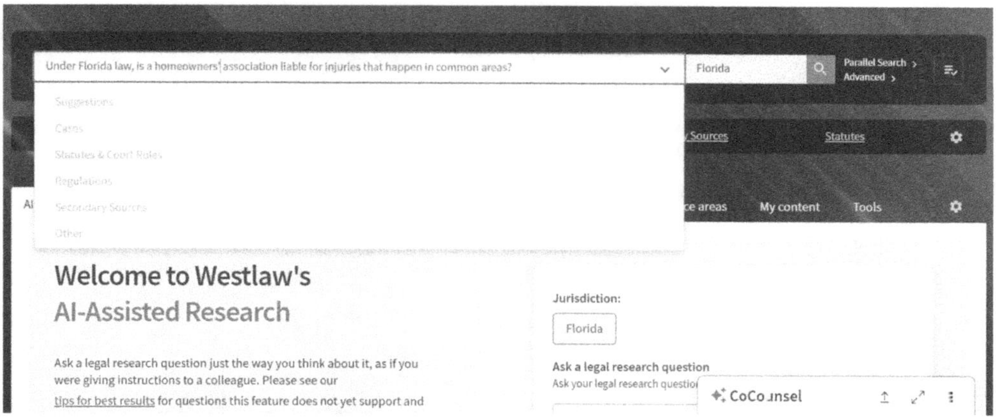

Figure 10.6 Legal Question #1

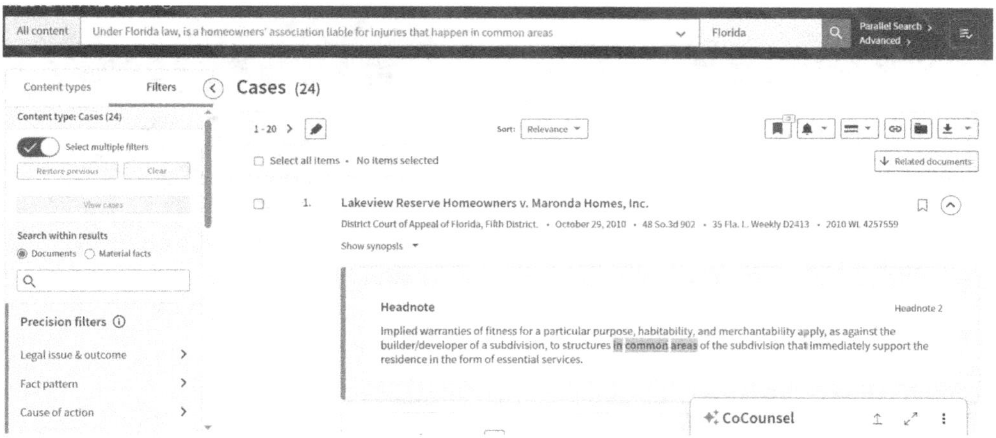

Figure 10.7 Response #1

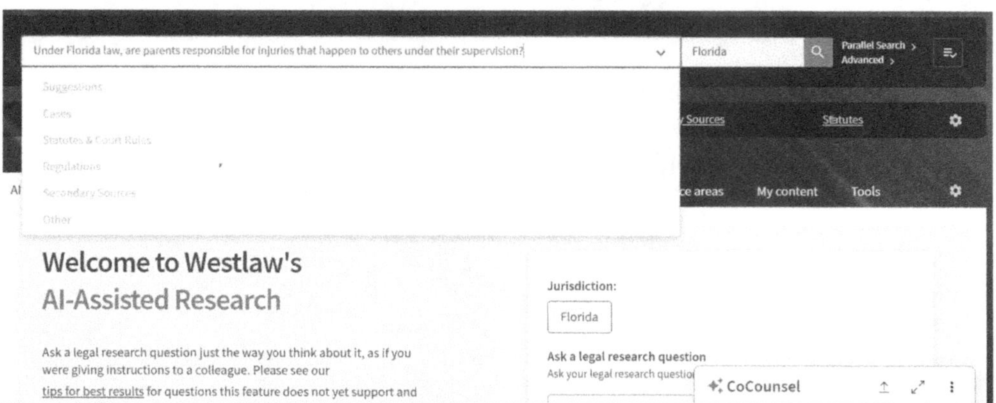

Figure 10.8 Legal Question #2

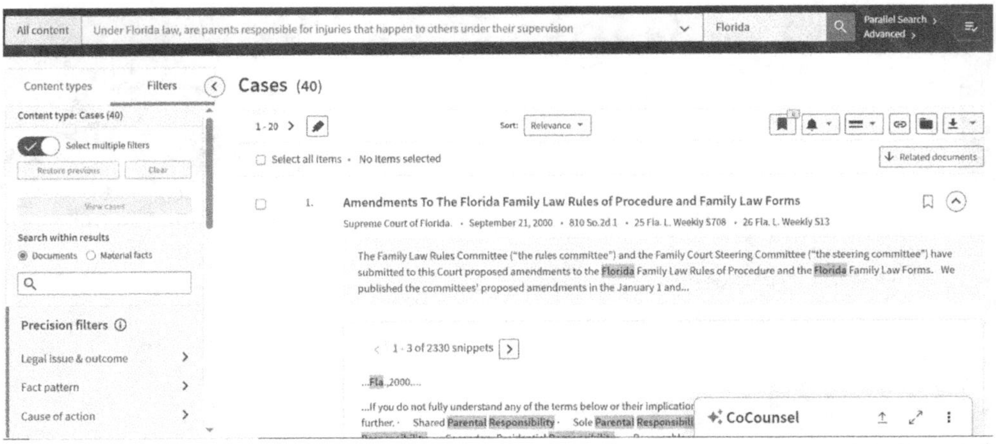

Figure 10.9 Response #2

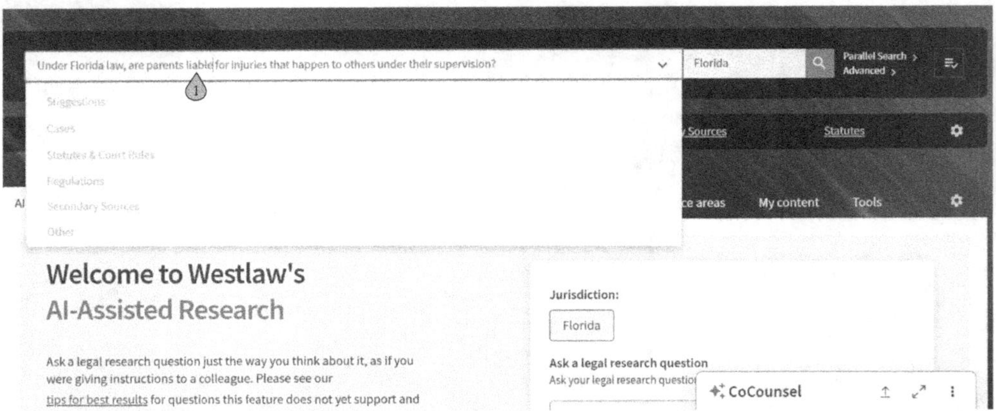

(1) "liable"

Figure 10.10 Refining the Legal Question

This question returned more case results as well as rules and regulations regarding family law. What would happen if we changed one word in the research question?

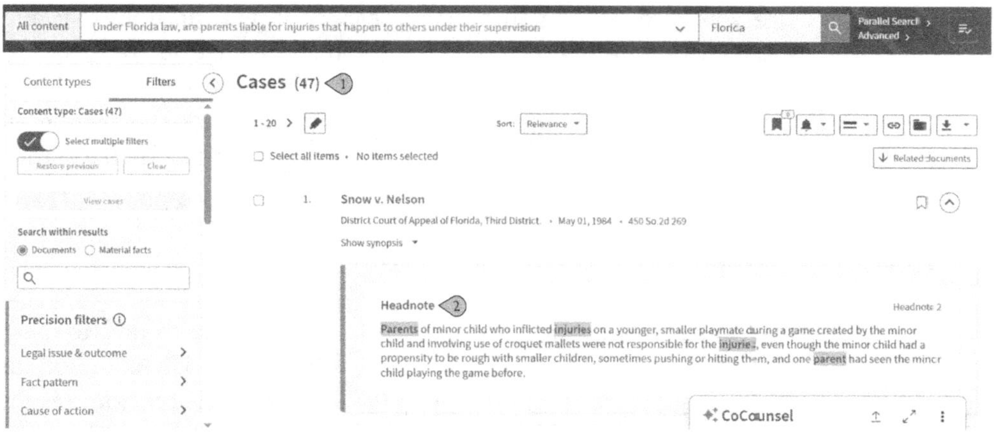

1 Cases (47) 2 Headnote

Figure 10.11 Response to Refined Legal Question

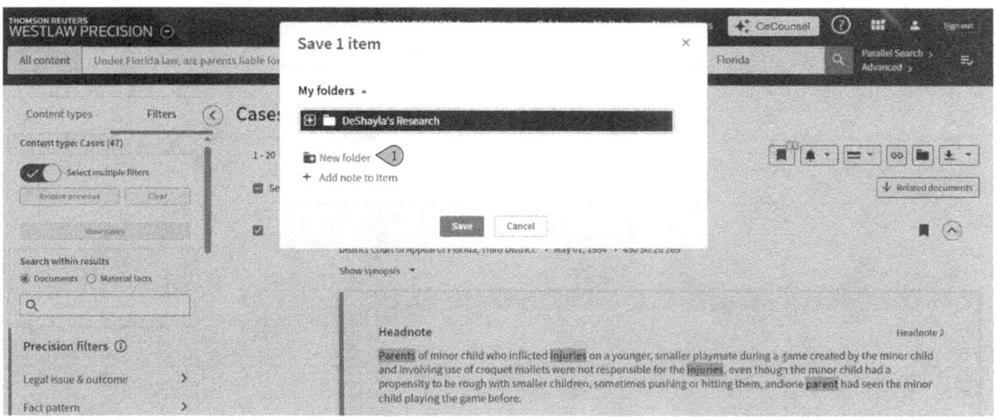

1 New folder

Figure 10.12 Create New Folder

Ahh, now we're cookin'! Swapping the word "responsible" with "liable" returned more results that also seem to be on point. The very first case shown here involves a playmate who was hurt during a game. From here, keep looking through results and refining the research questions. Now that we are starting to find helpful cases, it is a good time to create a folder to save these cases for later reference. You should also be adding the search terms and legal questions to your research plan. That way you can remember terms and questions that have already been searched. It may also be helpful to use case charts to help organize.

Once you have reached all possible relevant terms and questions and see the same cases and statutes repeating, you are likely done researching. You will want to establish the leading cases (the most cited cases) and make sure to prioritize binding authority. If you were not able to find an on-point case, remember to look outside the jurisdiction for persuasive authority.

Step 3:

Now that you have a pretty good group of cases, be sure to update them using citators in your chosen search engine. Citing good law is important to your ethics and representation. One of the cases from the previous results has a red flag. Click on the flag to review the negative treatment. Eliminate the case if it has been overturned on your particular issue. Remember that it may still be used for issues that were not overturned.

Just for fun, let's also check the Westlaw AI output for the same legal question.

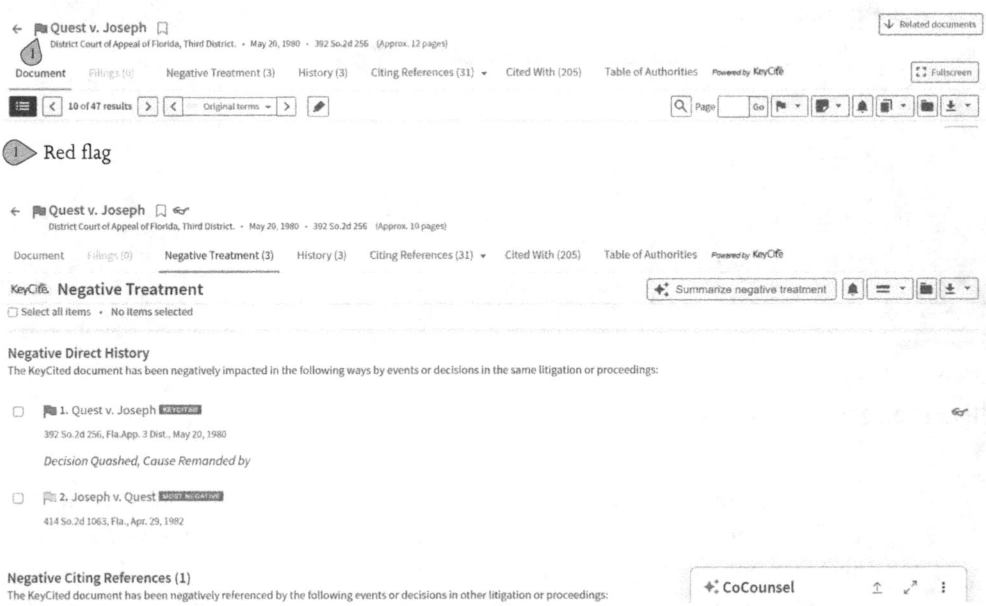

Figure 10.13 Checking for Good Law

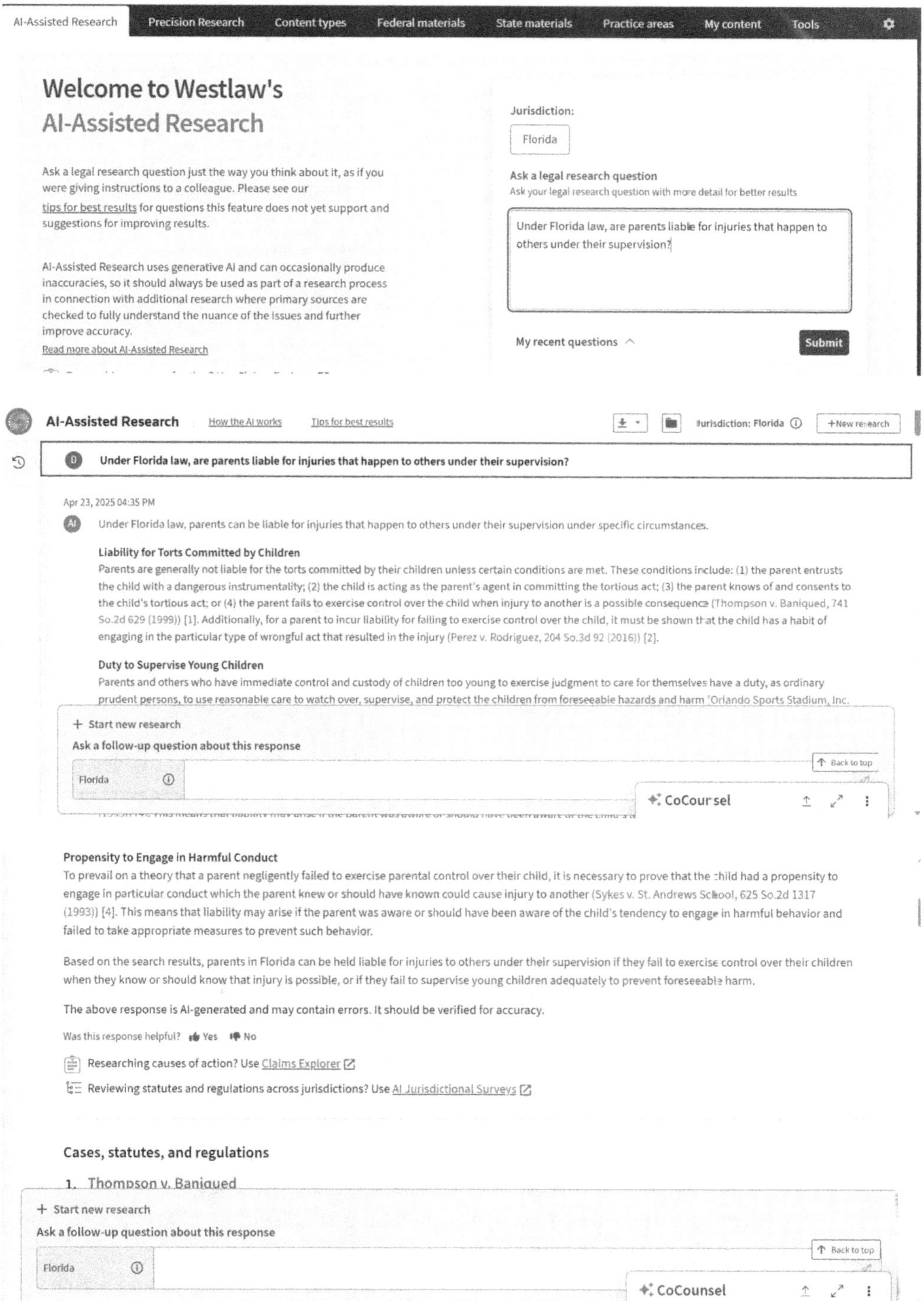

Figure 10.14 Using Westlaw AI-Assisted Research

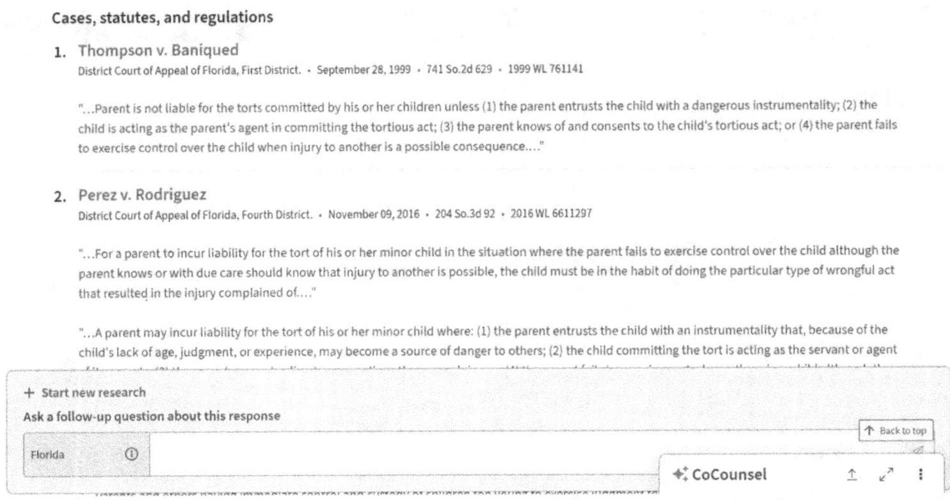

Figure 10.14 *Continued*

The AI search brought up seven cases as well as statutes and practical guides. Be sure to refine your prompt for an even more accurate output. And always check and double check AI output for accuracy. Only use AI on assignments if specifically allowed. Finally, you can pull the rules from the cases and apply them to your facts to answer the legal question(s).

CONCLUSION

Online legal research can be overwhelming at first, but it doesn't have to be. Practicing responsible research will set you up well to make effective arguments and to understand the foundations on which we practice law. Taking it step by step can alleviate the initial stress. Gather the information needed to start an informed search. That is where making the research plan with the who, what, when, where, and why comes into play. Gather the relevant legal material to help answer the legal questions. That may start with secondary sources but will lead to useful primary sources, which tend to be your most important allies. Update cases and statutes with citator tools to validate the law and ensure that it is still persuasive. Evaluate these legal sources for similarities or differences from your client's case. Use case charts and features charts to help organize your research.

These steps can make online legal research not only manageable but, dare I say, fun!

CHAPTER 11

Looking Ahead

THE FUTURE OF THE BAR EXAMINATION

The National Conference of Bar Examiners (NCBE) is an organization that attempts to promote fairness and best practices in admission to the legal profession. After much consideration, the NCBE announced that a new bar examination would be created to better reflect the evolving practice of law, with greater emphasis on assessing practical lawyering skills. Beginning in July 2026, the NextGen Bar Exam will replace existing bar exams in certain states.

Here is the current schedule for the rollout of the new bar exam:

July 2026:
Connecticut, Guam, Idaho, Maryland, Missouri, Northern Mariana Islands, Oregon, Virgin Islands, Washington

July 2027:
Arizona, Iowa, Kentucky, Minnesota, Nebraska, New Mexico, North Dakota, Oklahoma, South Dakota, Tennessee, Vermont, West Virginia, Wyoming

February 2028:
Delaware, District of Columbia

July 2028:
Alaska, Colorado, Florida, Georgia, Hawaii, Indiana, Kansas, Maine, New York, Ohio, Utah, Virginia

11. Looking Ahead

For the most up-to-date information, visit *https://www.ncbex.org/exams/nextgen*

The new examination will test research skills in a couple of different ways. According to the NCBE website, one way will consist of a performance task that will have a series of multiple-choice and short-answer questions followed by one extended-response question. For example, a performance task may include a family law scenario. Students will be provided with a file and a library, which is a packet of information that has all the family law rules necessary to give a complete answer. The file will contain a memorandum that describes the tasks. It may also include interview transcripts, depositions, or other documents. It is up to the student to know which rules from the library to apply to the given fact pattern. The exam will test foundational skills such as issue spotting, analysis, advising, legal research, and legal writing.

In short, the new exam has been designed to provide a more accurate and holistic assessment of the skills needed to succeed in the rapidly changing legal profession.

Legal research may also be tested in integrated questions. These questions are also based on a fact pattern and may include legal resources and supplemental documents such as e-mails, depositions, police reports, client interviews, etc. These questions will include a mix of multiple-choice and short-answer questions as well.

Examples

1. You are a state prosecutor. You have been assigned a case where a man shot into an occupied dwelling. He fled the scene going at least 80 mph in a 50-mph zone. State troopers stopped him for speeding. At the same time, the trooper gets a call to be on the lookout for a similar car and the suspect's description matched the man, the driver of the vehicle he currently had pulled over. The trooper walks back to the car and asks the man to step out of the vehicle. He steps out but starts to run before the trooper apprehends him and places him in handcuffs.

   Defense counsel has filed a motion to suppress the stop and detainment of the man.

   Which of the following legal topics is most important for you to research before appearing in court on the motion? Select two.

   a. *Miranda* warnings
   b. Reasonable searches and seizures
   c. Standing
   d. Arrest warrants
   e. Open fields
   f. Plain view

2. You have a client who was hurt on a cruise ship sailing from Florida to Mexico. She slipped on a liquid that was on the floor on the lido deck. Her hip and ankle were injured as a result of the fall. She wants to sue and get it over with as quickly as possible. She heard federal courts have strict deadlines and would be the fastest way to get it done.

   Your client seeks your advice on the best way to get this case into federal court.

   Which of the following search terms would be more likely to produce sources that will answer the client's question? Select one.

   a. Federal question jurisdiction
   b. Personal jurisdiction
   c. Removal
   d. Subject-matter jurisdiction

3. Section 7.3 of the statute does not define "nuisance." A partner at your law firm has asked you for guidance with defining the term in this jurisdiction for purposes of potential litigation.

   Advise the partner on two specific legal resources that are most likely to provide a controlling definition of "nuisance."

   (Enter short answer here.)

Explanations

EXPLANATIONS

1. The **correct** answers are **(b.)** and **(d.)** Partial credit is available for this question if at least one answer choice is correct. The stop of the vehicle and handcuffs triggers unreasonable seizures outlined in the Fourth Amendment of the United States Constitution. Placing him in handcuffs means the man likely did not feel free to leave or end the encounter, triggering more Fourth Amendment protections regarding arrests. (a.) Incorrect. *Miranda* warnings only kick in when a person is in custody and under interrogation. Here, there may have been custody but there was no express questioning or interrogation. (c.) Incorrect. Standing is required when one person is attempting to assert another person's constitutional rights. Here, there is nothing like that mentioned in the facts. (e.) Incorrect. The open fields exception to the warrant requirement triggers when the government is searching for evidence out in open outside areas that are easily viewable by any passerby. Those facts are not present here. (f.) Incorrect. The plain view exception to the warrant requirement is triggered when the police see contraband that is in their view when they are in a place they can lawfully be. Those facts are not present here.

2. **(d.) Correct.** Federal courts are courts of limited jurisdiction. Subject-matter jurisdiction is the court's power to hear certain types of cases in federal court. Because that is the advice the client seeks here, this is

the best answer. (a.) Incorrect. Federal question jurisdiction is a type of subject-matter jurisdiction that can get a case heard in federal court if the case falls under federal law. There is nothing in the facts that warrant federal question jurisdiction to be considered. So, this is not the best answer. (b.) Incorrect. Personal jurisdiction is the court's authority over the defendants in a case. This authority is required at the state and federal levels. Personal jurisdiction can be waived or consented to. A court may have personal jurisdiction, but subject-matter jurisdiction is still required to hear the case in federal court. So, this is not the best answer in this situation. (c.) Incorrect. Removal is a mechanism utilized to get a case from state to federal court. The defendant can file a removal if a case could have originally been heard in federal court. This is not the best answer because the plaintiff here is asking how to file in federal court at the outset of the case.

3. A "definitions" subsection within the same statutory scheme. Case law from a higher court in the jurisdiction that defines the term "nuisance" as used in the statute. The bar examiners are looking for specific examples of the types of sources that can be used to define an ambiguous word or term. Answers may vary.

   See other sample NextGen Bar questions on the NCBEX website, located at https://www.ncbex.org/exams/nextgen/sample-questions/.

APPENDIX A

Resources

Search Terms

Lexis—Search Commands and Connectors
https://www.lexisnexis.com/pdf/lexis-advance/terms-and-connectors.pdf

Thomson Reuters—Search with Terms and Connectors
https://www.thomsonreuters.com/en-us/help/westlaw-edge/searching/search-with-terms-and-connectors

Secondary Sources

Thomson Reuters—The Basics of Secondary Sources
https://legal.thomsonreuters.com/en/insights/articles/the-basics-of-secondary-sources-what-why-how

Thomson Reuters—Sources of Legal Research
https://legal.thomsonreuters.com/blog/sources-of-legal-research-primary-secondary-and-the-role-of-ai/

U.S. Library of Congress—Legal Research: A Guide to Secondary Sources
https://guides.loc.gov/law-secondary-resources

Citations

ALWD Guide to Legal Citation
https://aspenpublishing.com/products/williams-alwdguidelegalcitation7?srsltid=AfmBOor_h8f9zxwLtcX2Q3dTX6XuVx8Ywb4X6n2MtETX8649AtoTm8xZ

Introduction to Basic Legal Citation
https://www.law.cornell.edu/citation/

The Bluebook
https://www.legalbluebook.com/

Primary Sources

U.S. Library of Congress
https://guides.loc.gov/free-case-law/findlaw

FindLaw
https://caselaw.findlaw.com/

Justia
https://law.justia.com/cases/

United States Courts
https://www.uscourts.gov/court-records/find-a-case-pacer

Other Websites of Interest

OneNote
https://www.microsoft.com/en-us/microsoft-365/onenote/digital-note-taking-app

PowerNotes
https://www.powernotes.com/solutions/law

Unites States Courts
https://www.uscourts.gov/about-federal-courts/court-role-and-structure
https://www.uscourts.gov/about-federal-courts/court-role-and-structure/comparing-federal-state-courts

State Courts
https://www.courtstatistics.org/state-courts/state-court-structures

APPENDIX B

Lexis Search Commands and Connectors

Lexis Automatically Interprets Search Commands
Just enter your words and commands in the Lexis Search Box, e.g., ENTER: *drone and commercial W/10 deliver!*. **Commands are not case-sensitive**, i.e., enter AND, And or and.

Broaden W/N Connectors
While a Lexis search ignores certain "noise words" added to your search, it **counts all words** in results documents **for the purpose of determining proximity**. So broaden your W/n connector. In other words, consider W/10 instead of W/5. For W/p and W/s, consider W/75 or W/25 respectively.

Let the Advanced Search Help You
For help selecting connectors, select the Advanced Search link below the Search Box to access **Advanced Search** forms, which provide fields that help you use the right connector.

Common Legal Phrases
The Lexis service automatically recognizes many common legal phrases, e.g., *limited liability partnership*, *summary judgment*, and *search and seizure*. However, if you want to be sure any phrase you're searching is recognized, enclose it in quotation marks, i.e., ENTER: *"right to work."*

When More Than One Connector is Used . . .
Lexis acts on the connectors in this order:

- OR
- Proximity connectors (W/n, /p, near/n, etc. See next page.) from the smallest to the largest number value
- AND (You can use & instead of AND, except in legal phrases.)
- AND NOT or BUT NOT

For example, you ENTER: *bankrupt! /25 discharg! AND student OR college OR education! /5 loan*.

First, Lexis creates a unit of *student OR college OR education!*. Next Lexis joins *loan* with *student OR college OR education!* to create a unit. Then *bankrupt! / 25 discharg!* is joined to create a second unit. Finally AND (or &) operates last, joining the two created units.

Command/Connector	Overview
!	Child! finds child, children, childless, childish, etc. Used after word endings only. The word requires a minimum of three characters for the wildcard to be applied. Find the word root plus an unlimited number of additional characters. Note: Lexis automatically finds common plural words, i.e., ending in s, es and ies.
*	***When used as a suffix: Bank* is the same*** as **Bank! *The! and * are equivalents. They will both replace 0 or more characters when used with a three-character or more word root.*** Search results for bank* include bank, banks, banking, banker and bankruptcy.
?	***Lars??*** ***Bank???*** The industry standard ? replaces one character. For example, Lars?? finds Larsen and Larson. And Bank??? will find bank, banked, banker and banking but not bankrupt or bankruptcy.
OR	***physician OR doctor*** Lexis finds documents with either word or both words.
AND (or &)	***bank* AND deregulat!*** ***bank* & deregulat!*** Lexis finds documents with BOTH words only. Words can be ANYWHERE in the same document, not necessarily close in context. When entering legal phrases that contain AND, e.g., "cease and desist order," use "and" because Lexis is reading the phrase literally.
Proximity Connectors:	
W/n or near/n	***disparate WHO impact or disparate near/10 impact or disparate +10 impact*** (Use a number with W/n or near/n)
PRE/n or ONEAR/n +n, +s, +p	***cable PRE/1 tv OR television or cable ONEAR/1 tv OR television*** (The first word must precede the second within a specific number of words.)

Command/Connector	Overview
W/p or /p W/s or /s W/seg or /seg	Converts to W/75 Converts to W/25 Converts to W/100
NOT W/n or NOT /n	***disparate NOT W/10 impact*** finds documents where disparate is not within 10 words of impact. (Use a number with NOT W/n.)
AND NOT or % or BUT NOT	***rico AND NOT puerto or rico % puerto*** or ***rico BUT NOT puerto*** Lexis finds documents with "rico." Documents with any mention of "puerto"— anywhere in the document— will not be retrieved.
Special Commands: ATLEASTn	You must use a number and search words in parentheses with ATLEASTn. ENTER: atleast5(obama AND putin AND oil) and a Lexis search will find documents with at least five mentions of each search word. You can use the OR and AND connectors with ATLEASTn. You cannot use proximity connectors like W/n with ATLEASTn.
ALLCAPS	***allcaps(AIDS)*** You must use search words in parentheses with ALLCAPS. ENTER: ***allcaps(AIDS)*** and your Lexis search will find news documents with references to "AIDS" the acronym and ACQUIRED IMMUNODEFICIENCY SYNDROME but not "aids" the verb. NOTE: The ALLCAPS command works with news content searches only.
NOCAPS	***nocaps(aids)*** You must use search words in parentheses with NOCAPS. ENTER: ***nocaps(aids)*** and your Lexis search will find news documents with references to "aids" the verb but not "AIDS" the acronym. NOTE: The NOCAPS command works with news content searches only.

Command/Connector	Overview
CAPS	***caps(Rico)*** CAPS finds words with initial caps, e.g., proper nouns. You must use search words in parentheses with CAPS. ENTER: caps(Rico) and your Lexis search will find news documents with references to "Puerto Rico" but not references to the "RICO Act." NOTE: The CAPS command works with news content searches only.

APPENDIX C

Westlaw Power Searching and Connectors

Natural Language Power Searching

Natural Language: Not Just for Beginners

- You may have been told to use Natural Language searching because there is no special search method to learn; you just type your search in "plain English."
- You can become a Natural Language power searcher and achieve the most satisfactory results.
- Learn how
    - the document gets its final ranking in the results
    - to manipulate the terms in the search for the best results
    - to add alternative terms, including how to use the Thesaurus
    - to exclude terms from your search results
    - to conduct a field search in Natural Language
- Each document is given a score based on the document's statistical relevancy to the specific search.
- The score translates into the ranking of the documents in the result.
- The highest-scoring document ranks first and is displayed first.
- The other documents retrieved are displayed in descending order of statistical relevancy.
- Some documents in your results may not contain all, or even most, of your search terms.
- When you understand how documents are scored, you can manipulate your Natural Language search for the most successful results.
- Stop words (e.g., *the*, *is*, *for*) and stock phrases ("whether or not," "find all the cases that") are dropped from the query.

- Grammar is not important, but spelling is!
- The less often a term appears in a database, the higher it is scored, e.g., *Mazda* scores a 10, *car* scores a 1.
- Equivalencies are applied: *Avenue* = *Ave.*, *three* = 3.
- Special terms such as key numbers or citations are given greater weight.
- Westlaw uses the root word form of the term and then expands it similar to the way the "!" works in Terms and Connectors searches.
  - Expansion is more precise than the "!" in Terms and Connectors searching
  - create = *created creating creative*, but not *creature*
- Each document is then scored on the basis of
  - the score of individual terms from the query in the document
  - how many of the search terms are in the document
  - how often the search terms appear
  - how close the search terms appear to each other
  - the portions of the document in which the search terms appear
    - Example: Terms in the synopsis or digest field carry more weight than terms in the body of the opinion.

Manipulate Your Natural Language Results

- Place alternative terms in parentheses immediately following the original search term.
  - Grandparent (grandmother grandfather) visitation
  - You can use the Thesaurus feature or you can do it yourself.
  - The original search term is scored higher than the alternatives, but Westlaw recognizes that they are the same concept.
- Place terms of art and phrases in quotation marks.
  - Westlaw recognizes more than 78,000 terms of art and will add the quotation marks in Natural Language.
  - To be sure phrases are searched as phrases, put them in quotation marks.
  - The document is scored higher when the terms within the quotation marks are close together.

Manipulate Your Natural Language Search Results

- Repeat a critical term in the search.
  - The repetition won't show up as the search runs, but Westlaw gives additional weight to that term.
  - heroin (drug "controlled substance" cocaine) dealer dealer
- Include any unique (and relevant) term or phrase that will help your search retrieve on-point documents.

- For example, "social host" is almost always used in the context of a noncommercial supplier of alcohol whose guest becomes intoxicated and causes injuries.
- This high-scoring phrase will skew the results to retrieve relevant cases.

Control Concepts

- Control Concepts feature allows you to require that certain terms appear in each document or exclude terms from the documents retrieved.
- If you require that certain term(s) appear in each document retrieved, you might not get the maximum number of documents you chose: there may not be that number of documents containing that term(s) in the database.
- Be careful about excluding terms; this action can have unintended results.

Thesaurus

- The Thesaurus feature helps you select alternative words for the terms in your search.
- You can select as many alternative terms for as many search terms as you want.
- Click ADD, then OK to return to the search page with the modified search.

Field Restrictions

- You can restrict your Natural Language search results to cases from a specific court, or decided by a specific judge, or that have a specific attorney of record.
- You can restrict your results to certain dates.
- The fields available for use in a Natural Language search vary by the content of the database.

When to Use Natural Language

Use Natural Language searching when you are:

- not sure of the exact terms and need some flexibility when structuring your search
- searching in annotated statutes
    - Legislatures often use archaic, non-intuitive language.

- Language in the annotations often directs you to the appropriate statute.
- searching for broad concepts in any database
- searching in an unfamiliar area of the law
- retrieving too many or too few documents, or not the documents you need with a Terms and Connectors search.

Terms and Connectors Power Searching

Terms

- Use as many alternative terms as seem reasonable.
- Think not only of synonyms and acronyms, but also of antonyms and other terms that in the specific context might be used as reasonable alternatives.
  - intoxicated drunk inebriated
  - E.P.A. "environmental protection agency"
  - constitutional! unconstitutional
  - "social host" association club company
- The Thesaurus can help you with synonyms and sometimes acronyms, but it does not contain antonyms and other irregular alternatives so you need to add these yourself.

Expanders: Making the Most of Terms: The Root Expander (!)
Use as many alternative terms as seem reasonable.

- The root expander (!) retrieves all extensions of words with variant endings (up to 16 characters).

  drunk! retrieves *drunk, drunken,* and *drunkard.*

- Be careful not to truncate your root term too severely: **depo!** retrieves not only forms of *deposition*, but also terms such as *deposit, depositor, deposited, deport,* and *deportation.*

Expanders: Making the Most of Terms: The Universal Character (*)

- The universal character (*) is used in place of a letter (like a wild card or a blank tile in Scrabble).

  dr*nk retrieves *drank, drink,* and *drunk.*

- The universal character <u>cannot</u> be used in place of the first letter of a word.

- The universal character can be used at the end of a term to specify the maximum number of letters that may be added.

  object** retrieves *object*, *objects*, and *objected* but not *objective*.

Expanders: Making the Most of Terms

- You can use more than one expander in a term.
- s****holder retrieves both *shareholder* and *stockholder*.
- dr*nk! retrieves *drank*, *drink*, *drinkable*, *drunk*, *drinking*, *drunken*, and *drunkard*.

Terms: Automatic Enhancements

- The singular form of a word automatically retrieves the plural and possessive forms of the word, including irregular forms.
- The plural or possessive form of a word does not retrieve the singular form.
  - woman retrieves *women*, *woman's*, and *women's*
  - women or woman's do not retrieve *woman*
- Always use the singular unless you have a good reason not to do so.
- To turn off the automatic plural, place a pound sign before the word.
  - #damage (so you don't retrieve *damages*)
  - The pound symbol does not turn off possessives.

Terms: Automatic Enhancements – Imbedded Punctuation

- Statutes and Regulations
  - 415 retrieves 415 as well as 415.5 or 415(b), and 415.5(b)(2)(C).
  - 415.1 and 415(b) do <u>not</u> retrieve 415.
  - This is helpful when you are looking for mention of a statute that may or may not be cited to a particular paragraph or section.
- Dollar signs
  - $4000 does not retrieve 4000 or 4000.00
- Percent symbol
  - 50% does not retrieve 50 *percent*

Terms: Automatic Equivalencies

- Most variations of the spelling of a term retrieve other variations:
  - Judgment = Judgement
  - Millennium = Millenium
- Automatic equivalencies are built into Westlaw. For example:
  - Three = 3 – First = 1st
  - New York = NY – Avenue = Ave.

- To turn off automatic equivalencies, use the pound sign before the term.
  - #s.e.c. retrieves *S.E.C.* and *SEC* but not *section*

Terms: Other Enhancements

- Hyphenate compound words in your search.
- A hyphenated term retrieves the term whether it is one word, two words, or a hyphenated word.
  - good-will retrieves good will, good-will, and goodwill.

If you wonder whether a word is hyphenated, add the hyphen.
It can't hurt.

Terms: Other Enhancements

Use periods between the letters of an acronym to retrieve all of the following variations of the acronym:

- periods between letters
- spaces between letters
- periods and spaces between the letters
- no periods or spaces between letters

E.P.A. retrieves *E.P.A.*, *E P A*, *E. P. A.*, and *EPA*.

Connectors

Order of Processing

- The order in which Westlaw processes connectors can influence your results.
- But don't get too worried about the order of processing: follow your instincts and you'll be fine.

Order of Processing Connectors

- The general rule is that connectors are processed from narrowest to broadest: /s is processed before/p.
- The order: phrase, or, number, sentence, paragraph, and, but not
- The order: " ", space (or), +n,/n, +s,/s, +p,/p, &, %
- Connectors of equal value are processed from left to right.

Connectors Connect Terms to Form Units

The first connector processed will create a single unit, subject to the next connector processed.

- dog/s bit!/p yard
  - First Westlaw finds *dog* in the same sentence as *bit!*.
  - Then Westlaw finds that sentence unit in the same paragraph as *yard*.
- "social host"/s liab!/p injur!/s intoxicated drunk!
  - The phrase social host is processed first.
  - Then the space ("or") is processed.
  - Then the first/s is processed, creating a unit.
  - Then second/s is processed, creating a second unit
  - Then the first and second sentence units are found in the same paragraph.

Parentheses to Change Order of Processing (Nesting)

- Terms within parentheses are processed first as a unit that can change the order of processing.
  - dog/5 (yard/s bit!)
- First Westlaw looks for *yard* in the same sentence as *bit!*.
- Then that unit is found within five terms of *dog*.
- Useful when searching for alternative phrases
  - "products liability" (defect!/3 design!)/s windshield
- Useful when searching for multiple citations
  - (15 +5 1311) (42 +5 1985)

Phrases Within Quotation Marks

- Phrases are processed first.
- Stop words within quotation marks are processed as placeholders:
  - "accessory after the fact" also retrieves "*accessory before the fact*"
- You cannot use a connector within quotation marks
  - "Simon & Garfunkel" will not be processed
  - Try "Simon and Garfunkel" or Simon +2 Garfunkel

Numerical Connectors

- For the /n connector, *n* stands for a number between 1 and 250.
  - explorer/50 tire
    - Terms must appear within 50 words of each other; either term can appear first.

- The /n connector ignores grammatical units such as sentences or paragraphs.
- Use the /n connector when you want the terms to be close to each other but not in any particular order.

- limited/4 liability retrieves
  - *limited liability*
  - *liability was limited*

The Plus Connectors: +n, +s, +p

- The plus connectors require that the terms to the left of the connector precede the terms to right by a certain number of terms, in the same sentence, or in the same paragraph.
  - **homeowner +5 insurance** requires that *homeowner* must precede *insurance* by five or fewer terms. You will retrieve *homeowner liability insurance, homeowner fire and casualty insurance*, etc.
- The plus connectors are useful when you need a term to be repeated within a number of terms, a sentence or a paragraph.
  - **jones +s jones** requires that one *Jones* precede the other *jones* in the same sentence (*Jones v. Jones*).
  - **jones/s jones** requires only one *jones* be present in the sentence.

Connectors to Use Sparingly But When Needed

- The & (AND) connector requires the terms to the left of the connector be in the same document as the terms to the right, whether they are two terms or several hundred pages apart.
  - **good & faith** will retrieve many documents, not all of which will be addressing the issue of good faith.
  - You may have to use the & connector when it is the only way to retrieve any relevant documents.
  - The & connector must be used to link multiple fields together. Multiple fields are usually not in the same sentence or paragraph.
- **ti(honda) & at(john/3 brown) & da(aft 1995)**

Connectors to Use Sparingly

- The % (BUT NOT) connector
  - Add to the end of a query to exclude certain terms or combination of terms.

    d.u.i d.w.i. (driving +4 influence intoxicated) % "controlled substance" drug heroin cocaine
  - The above query eliminates any document that mentions any of the terms that appear after the % symbol.

- The query will also eliminate relevant documents that mention one of those terms in discussing analogous situations. Think of what you might be eliminating before using the %.
- You can use the % to eliminate documents with terms in certain fields.
    - **ti(honda) & sy,di(seat-belt) % sy,di(air-bag)**

Fields

- A field search makes your Terms and Connectors search more precise.
    - You are specifying which terms, the relationship between terms, and where the terms must appear in the results.
- Know which fields are available in the database you are searching: fields vary by content of database.
- You can create a combined field by manually placing a comma between the abbreviations of the fields you want to search with a single query.
    - **sy,di("wrongful death"/p insur!)**
    - **pr,ca("title 11" & "chapter 5" & exception/5 discharg!)**
- Westlaw field templates contain combined field text boxes for commonly combined fields, such as the ones above.

Fields

- You can create queries using multiple field with different terms in each field manually or by using the field templates.
    - The templates insert the "&" connector between multiple fields
    - The templates do not automatically add connectors within a field.
    - You need to add connectors within each field template text box **sy,di("wrongful death") & at(john/3 smith)**

Field Searches in Specific Databases

- In case law databases
    - **sy,di(grandparent!/s visit!)**
    - **wp("constructive notice")**
    - **sy(wilson) & sy,di("wrongful death") & da(bef 1999 & aft 1990)** (The name of the trial-level judge is often found in the synopsis field, especially in state cases where the trial level decision is rarely reported.)
- In statutes databases
    - **pr,ca("title 11" & exception/4 discharg!)**
    - **sd(penal! fine/s withdr*w!)**
- In news databases

- **ti("american motors")**
- **in(automobile) & da(4/10/2002)**

Locate

- Locate lets you browse your search results for particular terms, whether or not the terms appear in your original search.
- Locate Select **Locate in Results** at the top of the *Links for* tab.
- Locate in Result request always uses Terms and Connectors searching even if the original search used the Natural Language search method.
- You do not lose the results of your original search.
- When you use Locate, clicking the Term arrows takes you to Locate term(s), not the original search term(s).

Number of Documents in T&C Results

- Too many documents?
  - Use narrower connectors: use /s instead of /p
  - Search in a smaller database: use MN-CS (Minnesota Cases) instead of ALLSTATES (All State Cases)
  - Require additional (not alternative) terms
  - Limit search to specific field(s)
- Too few or no documents?
  - Use broader connectors: use /20 instead of /5
  - Search in a larger database: use ALLNEWS (All News) instead of MN-NEWS (Minnesota News)
  - Add reasonable alternative terms
  - Drop what was a required term
  - Try a Natural Language search

When to Use Terms and Connectors Searching

- Use Terms and Connectors searching when
  - you are searching for particular terms
  - you need a precise, controlled query
  - you are searching in a field(s)
  - you need to find all documents containing specific information, such as all cases with a particular topic and key number or all articles that mention a specific company name
  - you need to search a database for which Natural Language searching is not available

Index

www.ingramcontent.com/pod-product-compliance
Lightning Source LLC
LaVergne TN
LVHW082343200926
848481LV00012B/3434